Teaching Children
To Pray

Teaching Children To Pray

KEITH WOODEN
FOREWORD BY WESLEY L. DUEWEL

ZondervanPublishingHouse
Academic and Professional Books
Grand Rapids, Michigan

A Division of HarperCollinsPublishers

Teaching Children To Pray
Copyright © 1992 by Keith Wooden

Requests for information should be addressed to:
Zondervan Publishing House
Academic and Professional Books
Grand Rapids, Michigan 49530

Library of Congress Cataloging-in-Publication Data

Wooden, Keith.
    Teaching children to pray / Keith Wooden.
       p.   cm.
    Includes bibliographical references.
    ISBN 0-310-54481-5
    1. Christian education of children. 2. Christian education–Home
training. 3. Prayer–Christianity. 4. Family–Religious life.
I. Title.
BV1590.W66 1991
249–dc20
                                            91-34043
                                          CIP

All Scripture quotations, unless otherwise noted, are taken from the HOLY BIBLE: NEW INTERNATIONAL VERSION (North American Edition). Copyright © 1973, 1978, 1984, by the International Bible Society. Used by permission of Zondervan Bible Publishers.

Edited by Robert D. Wood
Cover designed by Tammy Grabrian Johnson
Cover and interior illustrations by David Slonim

Printed in the United States of America

92 93 94 95 96 / AF / 10 9 8 7 6 5 4 3 2 1

This book is dedicated to . . .
my daughter whose prayers humble and inspire me
my son whose spiritual inklings I adore
my wife who never stepped on a dream or crushed a fragile idea
and whose precious spirit nurtures a family for Christ

Their lives give me ample reason to pray and praise!

I am indebted and grateful to . . .
Becky Able, Tim Underwood, Judy Wagner, Nancy Wooden, and
Wilma (Mom) Wooden for reading, correcting, and critiquing the
original manuscript and whose input was indispensable
Wesley Duewel who has mentored so many, so incredibly,
through his books on prayer
Bob Wood whose keen care in editing and tenderheartedness
toward children put this book on the shelf

I am eternally in awe of God's great faithfulness

Little Jesus, wast thou shy
    Once, and just so small as I? . . .
Didst thou kneel at night to pray,
    And didst thou join thy hands this way? . . .
Thou canst not have forgotten all
    That it feels like to be small:
And thou know'st I cannot pray
    To thee in my father's way—
When thou wast so little, say,
    Couldst thou talk thy Father's way?
So, a little child, come down
    And hear a child's tongue like thine own;
Take me by the hand and walk,
    And listen to my baby-talk.
To thy Father show my prayer
    (He will look, thou art so fair),
And say: "O Father, I thy Son
    Bring the prayer of a little one."

   And He will smile, that children's tongue
      Has not changed since thou wast young!

Francis Thompson

Little Jesus, were you shy
 Once, and just as small as I? . . .
Did you kneel at night to pray,
 And did you join your hands this way? . . .
You have not forgotten at all
 What it feels like to be small:
And you know that I can't pray
 To you in my father's way—
When you were so little, say,
 Could you talk your Father's way?
As a little child, come down
 And hear a child's tongue like your own;
Take me by the hand and walk,
 And listen to my baby talk.
To your Father show my prayer
 (He will look, you are so fair),
And say: "O Father, I your Son
 Bring the prayer of a little one."

 And He will smile, that children's tongue
  Has not changed since you were young!

    Francis Thompson
    (An adaptation for today's child)

Foreword

Jesus loves our children. He loves to commune with them as well as with adults. He understands a child's mind and heart better than the parents do. He said, " 'Let the little children come to me, and do not hinder them, for the kingdom of heaven belongs to such as these' " (Matthew 19:14). Today he says, "Let the children pray to me." He rejoices to answer the prayers of small children.

How well I remember, long before I was able to read, placing my little red chair beside Mother's chair when she knelt in the kitchen to talk to Jesus. How well I remember the time I contracted scarlet fever and Mother reassured me, "Don't worry, Wesley, we'll just trust Jesus." Mother meant Jesus would take care of me. I understood her certainty to mean that Jesus would heal me as I asked him to.

The next morning the agnostic doctor could not believe his eyes when he returned and found me completely well. "Why! It must be wonderful to have a faith like that!" he exclaimed. Mother replied, "No, it is wonderful to have a God like that!" Then for an hour he listened and asked questions as Mother witnessed to him.

There is no greater way for Jesus to become real to a child than for the child to learn to pray to Jesus and to share his or her joys, disappointments, desires, and needs with him. There is no more natural way to learn that he is our Friend, that God loves us, and that God is real.

As our children pray, they come to know Jesus personally. They come to understand that Jesus cares, Jesus is with us, Jesus knows all about us, Jesus listens to us, and Jesus wants our lives to be pleasing to him. And somehow they also *experience* all of these truths, and they become wonderfully real to them.

Are you teaching your children to pray? This delightful book will challenge you to make prayer natural and thrilling in your children's day-to-day living. Keith Wooden writes from experience. This is not just theory; this is blessed fact. God can use this book to bless your home.

No child is too young to be blessed by the environment of prayer. The child who can understand the meaning of words can begin to understand the basic and simple essentials of prayer. These early experiences of talking to Jesus can lay the foundation for a lifelong meaningful walk with him—communing, interceding, and becoming mighty in prayer.

May God guide you to teach your children to pray.

Wesley L. Duewel
Greenwood, Indiana
November 7, 1991

Introduction

A BOOK ON PRAYER FOR CHILDREN

Mortified . . . with a grin. That would describe my wife's reaction. She was serving lunch to a group of pastors' wives at our home. My son, two and a half years old, bounded into the dining room just in time to hear Sherri offer to pray.

"I'll pray, I'll pray."

"Okay, Keaton, you may pray."

Keaton began with the traditional "bank-yous." His custom was to circle the table with his eyes, looking at each person and thanking God for individuals by name. It was one of those touching little characteristics that Sherri was eager to share with her friends. But suddenly his childhood prayer became a diatribe on dinosaurs, with names and demeanors shrilly set forth. Vivid accounts of dino demolition were recounted. Colorfully descriptive scenes were vocalized—with animation! Keaton had been watching one of the popular children's movies depicting the life of a little brontosaurus.

"De sharp tooth is berry, berry, berry . . . scaaaaary!"

Sherri interrupted twice with "amens," but they were premature in Keaton's mind. He had important things to tell God, and would not be distracted. Eyes flew open and a ripple of chuckles circled the table. Keaton ambled through more movie sequences from *Cinderella*, *An American Tail*, and *The Little Mermaid*.

Sherri's smile had turned to an impatient furrow, but Keaton began at last to wear down. Eyes closed again and with a bit of wistful reverence, the final amen was sounded and confirmed on several sides.

One person gasped, "You let him pray for *dinosaurs*?"

The truth is we didn't know how or even whether to stop him! But the question and the tone of the inquirer made us feel a bit uncomfortable.

If the truth be known, I am thrilled that Keaton and our daughter, Whitney, both love to pray. But maybe dinosaurs are out of the province of proper prayer. Or are they?

Perhaps prayer in the mouths of children is like sharp knives in their hands, simply not suitable until they are well taught. I can accept the conviction that irreverence is not to be countenanced. But was Keaton irreverent? If his prayer gave off the scent of undue familiarity, I could wish that all children were too familiar. I'm convinced that the heavenly Father must have welcomed Keaton's prayer as the fragrant incense it was. Our deep commitment to personal prayer and reverence for God would not allow us to let prayer degenerate into a flippant rehearsal of anything and everything that crossed one's mind. Certainly prayer is not child's play. *But prayer is definitely for children.* So how do you teach children to pray?

It was the faith, trust, and simplicity of a child that Jesus pointed out when he stated emphatically, " '. . . unless you change and become like little children, you will never enter the kingdom of heaven' " (Matthew 18:3). He spoke clearly when he held a child and said, " '. . . the kingdom of heaven belongs to such as these' " (Matthew 19:14).

It was as a child that I was taught to pray, and it was in prayer that I felt the first inkling of God. I worded my own prayer for salvation in simple children's terms—and nearly in the same breath asked God for a set of walkie-talkies. To me, He was interested in every detail of my life; and it never occurred to me that salvation and walkie-talkies were of qualitative difference to Him.

Because of my experience I want my children to pray.

One person quipped, "Not to worry. As long as teachers give math tests, children will learn to pray!"

Let me be more specific then. I want my children to pray not willy-nilly, but with direction and earnestness.

I want my children to love God as I love God. And if that means listening to dinosaur tales told in prayers, then for a season I will be comfortable with prayers for dinosaurs. Greater lessons are to be learned about God than simply that of proper subject matter and approach. Children must know that the God on the receiving end of prayer is a personal God.

14

But how do we teach them *how* to pray? How do we let them know that in prayer they experience the highest privilege given to us, the privilege of entering into the very presence of the Most High God? How shall they learn that prayer is the road back to a friendly relationship with him, restoring the intimacy that was broken (the most devastating part of the Curse), and that prayer opens the way for us once again to walk with God? It is the most privileged benefit of that intimacy. Oh, how I long to know that my children pray, that they know the privilege and power of prayer, that they know the presence of God.

In his book *All I Really Need to Know I Learned in Kindergarten*, Robert Fulghum salvaged from life's confusions the simplicity of childhood lessons—lessons so simple we have "outgrown" them, but we can never replace them:

> All I really need to know about how to live and what to do and how to be I learned in kindergarten. Wisdom was not at the top of the graduate-school mountain, but there in the sandpile at Sunday School. These are the things I learned:
>
> Share everything.
> Play fair.
> Don't hit people.
> Put things back where you found them.
> Clean up your own mess.
> Don't take things that aren't yours.
> Say you're sorry when you hurt somebody. . . .
> When you go out into the world, watch out
>   for traffic, hold hands, and stick
>   together. . . .
> And then remember the Dick-and-Jane books
>   and the first word you learned—the
>   biggest word of all—LOOK.[1]

I wish to recall for a moment the simplicity of my childhood—to return to the wisdom of the sandpile. I wish to climb into bed all snuggled and safe back on Hackberry Court—to hear the prayers I prayed with such faith and innocence. When did prayer become so difficult, so complex? When did I start referring to it as a discipline instead of a delight? I wish to recall the simplicity of prayer, rid of all its theological weightiness and "Christianese." Just for a time I'd like to be able again to pray like a child so that I can teach my children to pray.

Statistics tells us that we will invest $250,000 to rear each child, excluding college expenses. (Add another $250,000 by 2005 for college.) In this era of wise investment and maximum return, it is easy to see that our children will be our biggest investment of energy and time. If you're thinking cost accounting, it won't cost us a penny to teach them how to pray, but the investment continues from generation to generation (Psalm 78:5–7). This will be our *wisest* investment!

On the pages of this book you will find a tapestry (*hand*woven) of anecdotes from real life experiences, applied knowledge, and biblical wisdom on this matter of teaching children to pray. It is a path fraught with uncertainties. Bill Cosby stated in his book *Fatherhood*, "If God had trouble with His children, what makes you think it will be a piece of cake for you?"[2] Then he adds what most parents have also had occasion to say, "You know the only people who are always sure about the proper way to raise children? Those who have never had any."[3] I subscribe to that wholeheartedly.

Charlie Shedd recalls a lecture he used to give early in his career:

> ... with hopes they came for [my lecture] "How To Raise Your Children."
>
> Then we had a child!
>
> That sound you just heard was the great elocutionist falling flat on his face. My majestic speech (honest it was great) had been totaled. Those brilliant ideas had such a droll sound at two a.m. with the baby in full cry!
>
> In my defense I want you to know this: I kept trying. I changed my title to "Some Suggestions to Parents," and charged bravely on. Then we had two more children and I altered it again. This time it came out "Feeble Hints to Fellow Strugglers."[4]

When you write something about children, you feel that you need to be an authority. But no such animal exists. Certainly I'm not. Nothing written here is absolutely authoritative, save for God's Word. My words are born of simplicity, nurtured in experience, and delivered in honesty.

This one desire looms larger than any other concern: I want my children to learn to pray, not as a discipline but purely out of desire to speak with God.

Many years ago Jesus' disciples, having seen him pray regularly and so effectively, summoned their courage to make a request: " 'Lord, teach us how to pray' " (Luke 11:1, PHILLIPS). And he did! He taught them with words, but even more by actions like those recorded in Mark 1:35: "Very early in the morning, while it was still dark, Jesus got up, left the house and went off to a solitary place, where he prayed."

I hear a simple request that is on the lips of young disciples in my home. "Mommy, Daddy, teach us how to pray!"

Will we parents, grandparents, teachers, pastors do any less than what Jesus has done for us?

1
My Father Taught Me To Pray

My eyes are open, but they are not open for seeing. My room is dark. My parents have checked on me several times, as is their custom, and dutifully I pretend to be asleep. I'm listening—somehow having my eyes open helps me to hear. It is quiet except for one thing. I strain to listen to the voice from the next room. One thing of which I am certain, it is well past my bedtime.

A quietness settles over the house. Our place is accustomed to motion, constant motion, noise, and activity. Four children spread over fourteen years keep this house rocking. Silence ill becomes a home that usually quivers and shivers with the tumult of children at play. But the only thing running now is the furnace fan.

I wait.

My bedroom is next to my parents' room, and sometimes after I go to bed I listen to the voices coming through the wall. Tonight is such a night. I listen and I hear my father speak. The rise and fall of his voice is almost melodic. There are pauses and breaks, but the tone is steady. My father is praying, and I love to listen.

Now, if I'm honest, I'll have to admit that my motivation was not altogether from a pure heart in those days long ago. I wanted to hear my name. What would my father say to God about me? Would he be able to praise my behavior, or would his prayers rise nervously from an anguished heart? Children love to know someone is talking about them. You can almost watch their little ears perk up. I wasn't any different. You weren't either, were you? The more things change, the more they stay the same. Our daughter still loves to hear my wife and me talk about her. But

20

how could I have known back then that something much more profound was taking place? How could I have known that my father was teaching me to pray? In the quietness of our home on Hackberry Court I was learning lessons of prayer.

I do not recall this as a singular event but more as an accumulation of moments. Perhaps that is why they are treasured so much. I have prayers stored up for me over a lifetime. From my earliest recollection to this day, I can hear Dad praying.

He taught me to pray, but not as a conscious effort on his part. It was not by conventional teaching methods. No professional techniques here. I do not recall any learning objectives or lesson plans. Not one time did he give a quiz. He never taught me prayer construction. He . . . simply . . . taught . . . me . . . to . . . pray.

Bedtime prayers and mealtime moments are nice. In fact, they are very important. But if our prayer lives reflect only this ritualized commitment to prayer, we will never communicate to our children a lifestyle of prayer. It is sheer speculation, but I am convinced that many people have difficulty with Paul's exhortation to "pray without ceasing" (1 Thessalonians 5:17) because they have had modeled for them only the stated times and forms of prayer. They cannot imagine spontaneity in prayer. They have never seen it or experienced it. They have never known a moment when in the middle of an everyday event a prayer was spoken and God listened.

The centrality of prayer is learned more readily in the incidental and even accidental lessons than in the rituals of life. The way my father taught me to pray was shaped by his incidental approach to prayer.

In the conversations between God and Dad as he poured out his heart to his Father in heaven—from those I learned to pray. Great joy and praise found expression in his visits with our Lord. Sometimes his voice cracked and finally trailed off until he could recover his voice to continue his prayer. Occasionally he spoke no words, but I could hear the groans of the Holy Spirit as he poured out yearnings for his sons and daughter.

This is how my father taught me to pray.

Psalm 78:5–7 beautifully expresses what my father put into practice:

He decreed statutes for Jacob
and established the law in Israel,
which he commanded our forefathers
to teach their children,
so the next generation would know them,
even the children yet to be born,
and they in turn would tell their children.
Then they would put their trust in God
and would not forget his deeds
but would keep his commands.

A heritage from generation to generation—is that what my father began for his family in that room adjacent to mine? And has the baton now been passed to me so that I might pass it on to my children?

Let me make a tentative assertion. In looking back over my life, it seems that teaching prayer is not teaching a discipline; teaching prayer is *discipling*. It is echoing Jesus' call to the Twelve. In effect, we must say to our children, "Follow me!" It appears that the pedagogy of prayer or, if you will, the art of teaching prayer is for us to *live* prayer. Your children pay much more attention to your life than simply those formal times of talking with the heavenly Father.

YOUR LIFE AS THE PRIMER OF PRAYER

Do you recall your first grade reader? I'm a "boomer." I was reared on "Dick and Jane." An older generation grew up on *McGuffey Readers*. My daughter will be exposed to something like SRA (Student Reading Assessment). That doesn't sound so fun as "Dick and Jane."

Primers were our introduction to the world of reading. They taught us the fundamentals and exposed us to a world that was larger than we had ever imagined. What a delight those reading primers were! Reading gave us a window to life's variety and spice, opening to us unnumbered adventures. That is all well and good for reading, but, in case you haven't noticed, no primers on prayer exist, save one—YOU!

A dictionary definition of *primer* is "a small introductory book on a subject." You and I are that small introductory work on the subject of prayer for our children. Our lives are the primer on prayer. And our lives

22

are a book our children are certain to read, like it or not. You've probably heard the old saying, "Children have never been adept at doing what we say, but they are experts at doing what we do."

Don't let this scare you off! The requisites for being a prayer primer are amazingly simple. Gladys M. Hunt summed it up in *Focus on Family Life*:

> If your relationship with Jesus Christ is vital, your family will know it. They will know it not by your professional utterances, but by your love, your willingness to listen to ideas different from your own, your patience, your personal honesty, your obedience. It's contagious when it is authentic.[1]

Contagious authenticity is the only essential for becoming an effective prayer primer. It translates into flying the colors of your faith in life's everyday ups and downs.

One woman, whom I deeply respect for her attention to her children, explains the impact of her family heritage in this way:

> I was convinced that God lived in our house. Certainly in a sense he did, but early on I was convinced ours was his exclusive home. My parents talked to him constantly and in every situation—not so much formally but just conversationally. I learned to pray by talking to just another member of the household. I want my children to know God lives in our home, too.

Contagious authenticity! It is beginning to sound a little easier all the time—that is, until you see what it is your children catch from your contagiousness! We were rounding the corner by Aldi's food market—not the kind of place you expect to forge a profound analysis, but suddenly my daughter made a pronouncement.

"Dad, I've figured something out."

Every father thinks his child is gifted when he or she begins to "figure something out," so I was anxious to hear my daughter's insight.

"What have you figured out, Whit?"

"Well, God wants us to pray about big things and wants us simply to do the other stuff by ourselves."

At that moment I was considering jumping down some Sunday school teacher's throat for teaching my daughter such rubbish. Why would anyone rob my child of the delight of taking everything to God in prayer? Then I realized that *I am the teacher*.

"Where did you get that, Whit?"

"I just figured it!" (Oh, good, she doesn't suspect me!)

"Well, Whit, that's not really the way it's supposed to be."

Now Dad will not only have to make the correction here in words, but he will need to rewrite the primer of his life to reflect what he is telling his daughter.

If we are going to aspire to teach our children to pray, let's start with the essential. What do our lives tell them about our spiritual condition? Does the primer read that we live with God? My father's prayers were powerful, not because he was perfect—he wasn't—but because he was authentic before God.

When was the last time your children heard you pray other than at the regular times? Have your children ever seen you so moved in prayer that they saw your tears? Have they ever overheard their names in your prayers?

Keaton walked into the kitchen the other day while Sherri and I were praying about some personal hurts. Keaton is accustomed to seeing tears only when he hits his sister. He couldn't quite figure it out, but finally came to a conclusion and reprimanded us. "You guys stop fighting!"

I told him that we were not fighting, but praying.

I don't know about your father, but my father had a few proverbs that he would tell and retell—and retell and retell . . . *ad infinitum*. (I spent most of my high school years looking forward to college so I wouldn't have to hear those goofy sayings anymore.) One little parable/proverb he loved to tell was this: "Remember, Keith, life is like walking in snow. Wherever you put your feet there are some little feet putting their feet in your footprints."

You do not know how painful it is for me to repeat that—on two counts: (1) I vowed that once I got out of the house I would never have to hear that saying again, and (2) I now realize that it is true. It is profoundly true. We are the prayer primer of our children's lives. I can't predict how prayer will specifically flesh itself out in your life; I can only say that it must be fleshed out! Prayer must be a living part of our lives.

THE PRIMER SPELLED T-I-M-E

I recently attended a conference for pastors where I sat in on a seminar entitled "Prayer and the Success of the Pulpit." Only six of us were in the seminar (most were down the hall in "How To Grow a Megachurch"). I listened to the leader pour out his heart passionately on prayer. I was so touched by his obvious commitment to personal prayer as he spoke of his early morning disciplines and his watch-night vigils. His stature, in my estimate, rose to extraordinary heights. I am in awe of great prayer warriors. I long for that measure of spiritual growth in my life, but am often frustrated in pursuit of it.

Toward the end of his presentation he opened the session for questions and answers. Thinking of this book, selfishly I asked how he taught his children to pray. Pen poised to paper, I prepared to write feverishly. I wasn't even looking at him. I just waited for his answer—but the answer didn't come. The atmosphere in the room grew heavy, and I could feel the tension. I looked up to see him crying.

"I have four children," he hesitantly began. Then in one of the most painful moments in which I have ever participated, he said, "One of them died a few years ago. I think one of the others knows the Lord." He paused for a long time before adding hoarsely, "I don't know how you teach your children to pray."

It would be presumptuous for me to assume that I understood what he meant by saying he did not know how to teach children to pray. Without reading between the lines too much and placing exaggerated responsibility on this man's shoulders, I can say that I *think* I understood. Wasn't he saying that, despite the importance he had placed upon prayer, he had neglected consciously to teach his children to pray? It is possible to become so enraptured with the Lord that we ignore our family. It is even possible to walk in close communion with God at the expense of your family! Check out 1 Samuel 2:12–36 and see how Eli the priest learned that even service to the Lord can leave our families in jeopardy if we do not pay attention to the balance that God requires.

I venture onto this turf hesitantly and painfully. Still, if we are to talk about teaching our children to pray, it is ground we must cover. It seems

25

that the life paths of many great warriors of prayer are littered with the wreckage of their children's lives.

I heard Bruce Wilkinson address a congregation where he expressed my feelings with these words:

> I was on the East Coast at a secular meeting and someone came up and said, "Do you know who's sitting at the opposite table over there?" It was the son of one of our country's greatest spiritual leaders. Somebody whom, if I mentioned his name, you would all know.
>
> Well, I couldn't wait for break time. At break, I hustled over to him and bent down next to him and said, "I understand you're the son of so and so." And he said, "Yes, I am." Then I said, "What was it like growing up in the home of such a godly leader?" He pushed back his chair, stood up, and said, "I hate my father. I'm not a Christian; I'll never be a Christian." And he began to swear a blue streak. He walked out past me and walked down the hallway. . . . My expectations were here [pointing up] and reality in his life was here [pointing down].[2]

I know the man about whom he spoke. He was a spiritual giant. His life was a life of prayer. He would prostrate himself on the sands of Lake Michigan, crying out to God for his people. But his son hated him and his God.

If this were a pattern that everyone who wants a deep prayer life is bound to follow, I would be tempted to flee from prayer for the sake of my children. But it doesn't have to be.

Prayer closets are wonderful. Quiet times are essential if you are to hear God's voice. But these sanctuaries are not hiding places from our families. We can't afford to be so wrapped up in our own personal spiritual growth that we fail to develop our children's prayer lives.

In *Fatherhood*, Bill Cosby humorously writes, ". . . the father must have full-time acceptance of all the children. He must never say, 'Get these kids out of here, I'm trying to watch TV.' If he does start saying this, he is liable to see one of his kids on the six o'clock news."[3]

The same holds true in a much more serious way for our spiritual lives. Michael Webb beautifully made the same point in *Discipleship Journal*. "If [my children] come to me only to be turned away with the message, 'Leave Daddy alone! I'm being spiritual,' what am I communicating to them?" He adds that we need to provide "lap space in our Holy place."[4]

Nothing is more profound than the implications of that statement as we share our prayer lives with our children. A "prayer closet" that is open to the intrusive chatter of children may be the best opportunity you have to demonstrate your reverence and love for God. Invite them into your Holy of Holies to savor the presence of the Lord with you.

As you finish this chapter, take the pledge on these three things:

1. Let your contagious, authentic prayer life be seen by your children. Let them see and hear you pray. Allow your children to experience the sincerity of your prayers. Give them the sense that God does live in your house and with your family and that he is available to them.

2. Let them hear you pray at times other than bedtime and mealtime. Pray *out loud* and pray for them by name. Let your children relish the thought that you love them enough to bring them before your precious heavenly Father. They will catch the honor and warmth of feeling that this high privilege of their earthly father and mother talking to their heavenly Father about them will bring.

3. Prepare lap space in your holy place. Occasionally invite your children to share your quiet time, and never turn them away or hide from them. Even when they are uninvited, let them know that your time for God has enough room in it for a small child.

This poem reminds me of the heritage that I must leave by the example of my life—a heritage from generation to generation:

> *He carried it every Sunday,*
>   *as he walked the miles to church.*
> *Tucked in his pocket with hands*
>   *farm calloused and resting this day.*
> *The black leather cover*
>   *once stiff and glossy now worn*
>   *by caressing fingers*
>   *making it soft and supple as a hound's ear.*
> *He carried it after the pages*
>   *lost their starched crispness*

27

and the gilt was worn by years.
  And yet as limp and aged as it is,
    there's no greater treasure you could give,
    for within its pages is a man
    strengthened by hard work and a simple faith.
  I didn't know him, but as I touch these pages
    my hands become his hands and I can hear his prayers.[5]

Do your children ever hear you praying? I'm an adult now and have my own children, but in the vaulted chambers of memory I still hear echoes of my father's prayers.

AN EXERCISE IN PHILIPPIANS 2:12b–13

1. What opportunities do your children have to share informal prayer time? Practice this principle today.
2. Who "taught" you how to pray? Write a note to that person to express your gratitude; then add that you're now teaching your children to pray.
3. As you read this book, don't be afraid to use your pencil to mark places that speak to you. Mark prayer actions to incorporate into your family life, and record your thoughts in the margins.
4. Is your prayer life contagious? How does that contagion affect your children's health?

2
Pattern Prayers

Now I lay me down to sleep,
I pray the Lord my soul to keep,
If I should die before I wake,
I pray the Lord my soul to take.

You learned this prayer just as I did. Some well-meaning teacher or parent faithfully repeated it for us ever and again until we could recite it flawlessly.

Children love to hear the lyrical rhythms of rhyme. Who among us does not experience all over again ancient warm and fuzzy feelings upon recollecting lilting lines and vibrant imagery from Mother Goose? It was only natural that prayers find their phrasing in poetry. No doubt these pattern prayers introduce our children to the delight of rhyme. But to what else? Listen to those words: "If I should die before I wake. . . ." This childhood prayer and its "Friday-the-thirteenth" images must have scared many children half out of their wits! Think of the pictures that dance through their heads: ghoulish wrestling matches over their souls, gruesome death scenes such as the unprotected too frequently have seen on TV.

After this prayer, a child may be left with the feeling that every night bristles with potential danger. For kids who are convinced that things live in their closets and under their beds, this prayer could become fodder to fuel their worst nightmares. It is a prayer certain to scare the daylights out of any little kid. No wonder some want to sleep with the light on! There may have been a day when infant mortality and childhood diseases warranted a "comforting" prayer such as this, but today? Well, today some of us feel that it is hardly comforting.

I'm glad that we also learned other, less frightening prayers. You recall this one:

> *God is great, God is good,*
> *And we thank him for our food.*
> *By his hand we must be fed;*
> *Give us, Lord, our daily bread.*

How many can you repeat? Somewhere along the line someone spent a great deal of time and energy teaching you these little rhymes. You owe that person a great debt, and you can pay a bit of that debt by rehearsing those prayers now. Like the Gettysburg Address you learned in the seventh grade, once you have learned these prayers they are yours forever.

When the childishness of these rhymes wore thin, some of us replaced them with adult versions of pattern prayers. "Bless this food to the nourishment of our bodies," can be uttered at breakneck speed. Even if they are not memorized rhymes, we still have our hackneyed phrases in prayer. I hope that they don't degenerate this far:

> *Dear Lord,*
> *Bless my life,*
> *Bless my wife,*
> *Our son, Red,*
> *And his wife, Deb,*
> *Us four, no more.*
> *Amen.*

Who among us has not embarrassed himself or herself completely by giving the "right" prayer at the wrong time? Blessing food at a bedtime or bedtime prayers at breakfast (obviously before the morning coffee). We know them; we just get mixed up on when to use them. Pattern prayers are a segment of our social religious heritage, but they may need some evaluation.

30

THE PROBLEM WITH PATTERNS

Pattern prayers are those prayers we have learned by rote. Do children learn them because we are so dedicated to teach them, or are they really beneficial to young children beginning to pray? Maybe these patterns are only the *rudiments* of prayer, foundations that children can learn and then use later as a base for their own formulations. If so, we can compliment ourselves. But if they are not foundational, then maybe they are simply inadequate.

Even the Lord's Prayer, taught as a pattern prayer to youngsters, can confuse them. One little girl returned from visiting her friend and told her mother that Janie was *so* lucky. When her mother asked why, Sarah explained, "Because God and the Holloways have the same name."

"What do you mean?" asked the mother.

"You know, in the Our Father prayer. 'Our Father, who art in heaven, Holloway be thy name.'"

Pattern prayers emphasize form, not function. Greater attention is given to the proper word, rhythm, or rhyme than is given to the prayer's relevance to the child or comprehension by the child and the child's mode and sincerity of expression. But pattern prayers have an even more serious effect. Memorized prayers can rob our children of essential aspects of their relationship with God. These essentials will be hard to put back into that relationship later in life. It is even possible that pattern prayers may rob our children of some of the most precious elements of prayer. Possibly such prayers could even hinder children from developing genuine, warm, saving relationships with a loving heavenly Father, which is the purpose of prayer.

THE PRACTICAL PURPOSE OF PRAYER

You've heard the story of the little girl who was rushed off to bed with the admonition, "Don't forget your prayers." The next morning her mother asked whether she had remembered to pray. The child explained, "Well, I got down on my knees and started to say them, and all of a sudden I thought, I bet God gets awfully tired of hearing the same old

31

prayers night after night. So I crawled into bed and told him the story of the three bears instead."[1]

Can't you imagine how amusing it would have been to be just outside the door that evening to hear a small child entertain God: "... and Goldilocks said, 'This bed is too hard.'" If it makes a father like me smile, picture the face of our heavenly Father.

Rather than the recitation of rhymes, this little girl discovered a personal God—a God who hears not just the words, but the heart of a child eager to share her most precious story. This is the kind of child who was rebuked by the disciples but welcomed by Jesus.

The children of Jesus' day were no less childlike than children today. Probably the disciples shuddered when they thought about what those little urchins might say, how trivial their questions, how silly their prattling. The least their parents could have done was to coach the children in the proper approach to so great a teacher. But that is not what Jesus wanted. He wanted *them*! Unrehearsed. Inimitably natural. In a word, *themselves*.

Children, who in a group look more like writhing worms than attentive students, seem able to cut through all the religion talk and etiquette, and approach the throne of God with simple eloquence. They touch the heart of God because nothing stands between their hearts and his. No charades or masks. No pretense or sophistication. Just unrehearsed, unadorned children. Listen to them pray sometime. If Jesus is interested enough to sweep them up in his arms (see Mark 10:13–16), isn't he delighted to listen to the story of the three bears? What do you think?

Unwittingly, this child understood two significant lessons of prayer—lessons as simple as sandbox wisdom but as crucial as God's Word itself—lessons often lost in pattern prayers. These are foundational lessons to be rehearsed and reinforced.

The two lessons? *God is personal. God cares for persons*—as individuals not in clumps.

PRAYING TO A PERSONAL GOD

We live in a mechanized society. Twenty-four-hour tellers are not tellers at all; they are machines. Computers dial phone numbers with

33

prerecorded messages. Telephone-answering machines respond to prerecorded messages with prerecorded answers. So much for reaching out and touching some*one*. Some children are better acquainted with mutant turtles or a Mario Brother than with their parents. After all, with whom do they spend more time in a given day?

It is not a distant journey for a child to see God as controlled by a joystick rather than his being in control. God can easily be conceived of as a vending machine or a video game: action (prayer), reaction (answer). Some adults seem even more prone to reduce God to a celestial satisfier. We lose our perspective. We confuse God's role with ours. It is his job to glorify humankind and satisfy our desires. I do not condemn pattern prayers wholesale, but I do believe that they tend to stifle spontaneity and freedom so that we cannot and do not give expression in our praying to our true feelings and concerns.

I love the lesson a child taught his father as they prayed together. After the father prayed, his son began to pray. He spoke quietly, almost inaudibly, to his Father. Annoyed, Dad interrupted, "Son, speak up, I can't hear you."

"That's okay, Dad; I'm not talking to you."

The most valuable lesson we teach our children is that it is *God* to whom they are speaking.

This goes double for parents who try to set an example in their praying. Listen closely to yourself. Who is your intended audience? Are you rehearsing your child's bad behavior and asking God please to help Johnny be good? If your children get the idea that your prayers are your way of letting them know you don't approve of their behavior, your way of scolding by way of the backdoor, your way of making pronouncements, they will take note. Prayer, they will conclude, is not really talking with God; it is a useful and safer way for people to talk to each other. That is, indirectly. In prayer we jab, cajole, reprimand each other, sometimes with barbs and with no opportunity for rebuttal, and all under the guise of talking to God. (You've undoubtedly heard scoldings, belatedly remembered announcements, and sermonizing in public prayers.) Your children will resent the lesson, and will realize that you have not really spoken with God in your prayer. You have really been talking to them.

If we are going to teach personal prayer, make sure your prayers model that intimacy and that they are not something else under the guise of prayer. The blessed privilege of talking with God about them or on their behalf is not to be prostituted by using your prayer as a club.

Do not be overly concerned about details of your prayer or "correct" form as you begin to model prayer. Over time children will learn appropriate concerns in prayer, and the issue of dinosaurs and other childish fantasies will eventually take care of themselves. God certainly will not be offended, so why make an issue of such delightful innocence? Teaching children to pray may sound simple, but it is not simplistic. Our Lord cares about any event or situation that is important to your children. The critical matter is for children to learn that there is a personal God who cares personally.

MAY I SPEAK TO GOD, PLEASE?

I hear adults talk about the discipline of prayer. I recoil when I hear prayer listed as a discipline. Prayer becomes a discipline when it has been robbed of its heart, which is *relationship*. Is it a discipline when words tumble over one another as we tell a friend of an important experience we've just had? Is it a discipline when a child's exuberance spills over into laughter and energy? If a child has been introduced to a personal God, a God who through Christ referred to us as friends, then prayer will never be reduced to a discipline. Listen to a child pray who has never been "taught" how to pray. The thank-yous trip over each other.

When Jesus blessed little children, it was not at arm's length. We must not keep them an arm's length from him today. Let them come close. "'Let the little children come to me, and do not hinder them'" (Mark 10:14). And what did the Shepherd of our lambs do at that point? ". . . he took the children in his arms, put his hands on them and blessed them" (v. 16). What a tender and lovely picture that is!

A GOD WHO CARES FOR YOU

Let's stress relationship, not mechanics as we teach our children to pray. Every child has a friend. To our great misfortune and disgrace, the terms *mother* and *father* in today's society carry emotional baggage that

35

can be destructive, but every child has friends. Since Jesus called us friends, teach children that God is their friend. This helps regardless of the sociological makeup of the family.

What do friends say to each other? What do friends share that they would not unburden themselves about to anyone else? Well, that's what our Lord wants to hear: their songs, their thoughts, their joys, and their hurts. For this reason I would not discourage children in any expression of what is on their little hearts, no matter how inappropriate that expression may seem to me. Just as I choose to try never to embarrass children in front of their friends, so do I allow great latitude in prayer. Time will teach children what is appropriate in prayer as they listen to your prayers and watch your life.

Someone overheard a four-year-old reciting the alphabet to God, which he had just learned—hardly a tip-off for the Most High but to the child the greatest treasure trove of the day. When questioned as to why he divulged the information to God, the little boy responded, "I just said him the alphabet, and he can put it together the way he wants."

Relationships with friends, of course, do not fit at all into fixed patterns. Just as it would be ridiculous to teach our children a standard recipe for interpersonal bonds, it is obvious that if we are going to teach our children to relate to God, in a personal and interpersonal way, any formulas are going to fall short. But some are still going to ask, "Well, then, how? How do I teach my children to pray? What do I encourage in their prayers and what do I discourage?" Aside from giving them great latitude to talk freely with God, some guidance will be helpful. In that case, a human-relationship model, inadequate as it is, should be adopted.

A PATTERN WITH PERSONALITY

Some parents will not like the idea of throwing out, lock, stock, and barrel, the idea of memorized prayers. We all know that children get the "bank-you" prayers right away. "Bank you" for food/dog/cat/grass/bike—you name it. Sometimes I watch my son praying and he opens his eyes, just looking around the room, taking in whatever looks like something to be thankful for. These prayers give way to thoughtful prayers soon enough. Children will naturally desire more insightful prayers as they relate with greater understanding to their world. This is the time perhaps to introduce more.

As I say, I have reservations about pattern prayers. But if a memorized prayer helps the young pray-er, then, in balance, it will be of some value. But if I'm going to recommend a pattern, it must be the least obtrusive pattern possible, one that retains personal expression with a personal God. It must be only a guide and not a generic roadmap, as if one map will show the way to all destinations.

I suggest the five-finger prayer pattern, which has been around for many years. It guides without throwing up roadblocks, and it is simple enough for a child to learn.

Have your child place his hand on the table or bed, and illustrate the following to him or her:

1. *Your thumb is close to you so it will represent those who are close to you. It reminds you to pray for your family members, relatives, and friends.*

2. *Next comes your pointer finger. This finger reminds you to pray for people you want to point to Jesus.* (It is surprising how perceptive a child is about those who know Jesus in their hearts and those who do not. Let them name those for whom they're praying. In the chapter "Letting Them Touch Their World Through Prayer," I relate the miraculous way this has affected our family's prayer life.)

3. *Your third finger represents those who are in authority. It is the biggest finger and the strongest one. It stands for leaders, pastors, missionaries, teachers, and "big" people for whom you want to pray.*

4. *The fourth finger is your weakest finger. It reminds you of people who are weak, sick, or going through difficult times.* (My daughter saw a person on the street who was homeless, and she wanted to pray for his needs. Do not press children to pray in this area. Let them pray as they become aware and concerned.)

5. *The smallest finger reminds you to pray for yourself.* (It helps children place their own needs in perspective.)[2]

Children who are prepared to pray do so more thoughtfully. Before they pray have them think about some of the important things they want to pray about. Sing a couple of songs they like to prepare them for conversation with God. Remind them that it is he to whom they will be talking. I am often guilty of tickling and teasing at bedtime and then expecting my child to make a flip-flop in emotions as we begin to pray. Unfair. Prepare for prayer.

If children come into their room at full speed and, because they are excited and playful, simply crank out a prayer, they are not going to sense in any way the significance of a personal God.

Also, if you rush your children through prayer so that you can make it back to catch the rest of your TV program, your priority will not be lost on them; they will be certain to sense that for you TV is more important than talking with God. Prayer takes time. So take the time!

John Drescher relates an incident in his family that brought home the importance of worthwhile time with his child. He wrote:

> One night I was about asleep when I heard the footsteps in the hall. Three year old David came slowly through the doorway and stood by my bed.
>
> "What do you want, David?"
>
> "Nothing, Daddy. I wanted to crawl in beside you and talk a little."
>
> I pulled the covers back and in he came. He snuggled there in silence a short time and then said, "Daddy, it was fun holding your hand in front of that lion's cage today."
>
> "It sure was. Were you scared?"
>
> "Just a little."
>
> After another short time of silence, David said, "We really had a good time together today, didn't we, Daddy?"
>
> "We sure did."
>
> And that was all. David threw the covers back and went quickly into his own room. He was soon sound asleep. But I remained awake for some time. My small son awakened me anew to the importance of taking time to be together as a family.[3]

Tonight, when the lights are turned out and your children are snuggled in, listen to them. Forget about TV. Ask them, "What do you want to pray about tonight?'' Chances are that they will tell you, and in the process you and they together may discover all over again a God who is personal and personally interested.

AN EXERCISE IN PHILIPPIANS 2:12b–13

1. Listen to your children pray a pattern prayer and then check to see how much they understood of that prayer. For example, what does ''by his hands we must be fed'' or ''hallowed be thy name'' mean to them?
2. If your children prefer pattern prayers, encourage two prayers: a set one and one of their own.
3. If you make a practice of ''talking'' your children through prayer, encourage them to speak to God for themselves.
4. Experience the awe of considering the One to whom your children are talking and of how much he cares for them.

3
When You Lie Down ...

Love the LORD your God with all your heart and with all your soul and with all your strength. These commands that I give you today are to be upon your hearts. Impress them on your children. Talk about them when you sit at home and when you walk along the road, when you lie down and when you get up.

(Deuteronomy 6:5–7)

In Edith Schaeffer's *L'Abri*, she describes her life and that of her family as they lived under the scrutiny of a few people who were on their first trip abroad and who found shelter (that's what *l'abri* means) in their Swiss home. Then the Schaeffers became well-known internationally and had to live out their lives under the eye of everyone in the known world. She reared her children in an intellectual environment where university student skepticism freely questioned every philosophical and theological assumption. Provocative discussions took place daily in quiet chalets at the base of the Swiss Alps. As I read her account of the Schaeffers' life, I paused upon simple words that made me wonder whether in them lay the essence of living and of bringing children to an acquaintance of spiritual reality.

The thing about real life is that important events don't announce themselves. Trumpets don't blow, drums don't beat to let you know you are going to meet the most important person you've ever met, or read the most important thing you are ever going to read, or have the most important conversation you are ever going to have, or spend the most important week you are going to spend. Usually, something that is going to change your life is a memory before you can stop and be impressed about it. You don't usually have a chance to get excited about that sort of thing . . . ahead of time![1]

What simple and sensible eloquence! Is there a better summary of the way we live? To a degree, we live our lives with one eye always on the rearview mirror. It is only in the mirror that we see an event for what it really was. Experiences usually go unnoticed at the time, but suddenly in the image in the mirror we see a "historical marker" that explains significances. It is only in reflection that we have a chance to experience the impact of an occasion. This is especially true when we speak of our children. Teaching times with children don't come in neat packages. They don't announce themselves as the "perfect moment." Often there is no hint that the opportunity has ever risen until afterward, at the end of a day, as you find yourself drifting into semiconsciousness. Or maybe that insight doesn't come till the end of a decade. Maybe only then do you understand the moment for what it was, that you could have said something to strengthen your child's faith—or to build his or her self-esteem. And if you responded well at the time, you thank the Lord for using you as his instrument to help your child.

All this talk about "quality time" is extolled generally only by those who are unwilling to give themselves unstintingly to and for their children. To speak in terms of quality time is really only an effort to justify a lifestyle that leaves little room for a genuine commitment to parental responsibility and opportunity. There is no such thing as quality time without the investment of a quantity of time. You do not schedule first steps and scraped knees. A teardrop will not wait for a convenient time. Quality time and quantity time become synonyms. We cannot even hope to influence our children unless we are willing to expend expanses of time with them.

Perhaps it goes without saying that children can see your faith only if they can see you physically present with them.

In a card shop, my daughter came upon one she thought was pretty. She said to her mother, "Let's send this card to Daddy, to tell him how much we love him." Speaking from experience, when your child thinks of using the postal service to get in touch with her father, you realize you have been away from home too long.

Our children must be our priority. God forgive us—God forgive me—for there have been times where I have regarded a trivial TV program as more important than the request of a child. Even a program with lasting and redeeming value must take second place when viewing it deprives children of the attention they need. When the drone of my children's *whys* and *whats* have got to me so much that I tune them out and attend to my own interests over theirs, I need to take stock of myself once again. (I must add that, of course, those times arise when my concerns must take priority over the children's, but I'm talking about *habitually* neglecting my children because I'm too self-centered to give them the attention they have a right to expect.) Dr. Howard Hendricks has said that the home is still the number one influence in the child's life. "The average church has a child one percent of his life, the home has him eighty-three percent, the remaining sixteen percent is spent in school."[2] These statistics do not minimize the need for our churches and our schools, but they do maximize the importance of the family and parental and sibling impact upon children. If we parents are really eighty-three percent of our children's world, that fact plants firmly in our minds that we must attend to our responsibilities. Among those responsibilities is our unparalleled opportunity to teach our children to pray.

I remember the cartoon by Ernest Lewis of a boy who approached his father with his grade card. I could tell from the expression on the father's face that the report was less than acceptable. With a scowl the father was about to blast his child when the quick-witted little fellow asked a relevant question: "Dad," he asked, "what do you suppose it can be? Is it heredity or environment?"[3] Dad was definitely put on the spot. He had left his mark on his son, and he was responsible for his influence.

As a Christian, you cannot wash your hands of your parental obligations. You are going to make an impression on your children, by heredity or environment or both. In fact, you have to keep your hands soiled with your children's needs—involved all the time right up to your elbows. No, right up to your heart.

The Scriptures are clear at this point. God emphasized this matter centuries ago when he spoke to the Israelites. He told his people that they had awesome responsibility to and for their children. And he allowed for no exceptions. Consider what he said:

Love the LORD your God with all your heart and with all your soul and with all your strength. These commandments that I give you today are to be upon your hearts. Impress them on your children. Talk about them when you sit at home and when you walk along the road, when you lie down and when you get up (Deuteronomy 6:5–7).

When God gives a priority, he also provides a plan. Deuteronomy presents to us an outline of how we are to affect our children in their spiritual life. We are invited—no, obligated—to become heritage makers, moms and dads not only physically or through adoption, but also moms and dads through whose influence our children are born into the kingdom of God. It is a matter of injunction, indoctrination, and integration.

INJUNCTION

The words of Deuteronomy 6:4 were recited each day by the Israelites. It was called the *Shema,* which means "hear," with the clear implication of hearing and obeying. Faithful Jews repeated it every day. It was the creed of Israel: "Hear, O Israel: The LORD our God, the LORD is one."

Look again at verses 5–7 quoted above, and note the number of personal pronouns. *You* is mentioned five times. This is not a message for someone else. God had this written just for you, and you can't escape its directness. You can hardly read it without thinking of the words of Elizabeth Barrett Browning, which she wrote in a different context: "How do I love thee? Let me count the ways." Deuteronomy speaks of three exhaustive ways in which we can measure how we love God—three ways, no more, no less, because they encompass the whole of our affections. He defines the boundaries of our love. Love must characterize our heart's desires, our soul's interests, and our strength's embrace. Our love for God must saturate our being. We must never reduce that love to mere ritual, a "religious" obligation; it is our work to keep love sparkling with vitality, a firsthand faith. It won't matter how loudly you play your faith for your children. If it is not authentic, they will not hear it.

Someone has said that character is what we are when no one is looking. *Faith* can be defined similarly. What definition are you giving to faith when your children are watching? Far too often there is a

43

discrepancy between our public profession and our private faith. Don't think for a moment that it escapes the eyes of your children.

Is your faith hollow, superficial, half-hearted? Don't even think of passing that kind of faith on. But, sadly, if that is true of us, then that's all we *have at our disposal* to pass to our children. The injunction is for us first to evaluate our own lives in light of our love and devotion to God. If your faith is upon your heart, if it is deep and genuine, then you have a calling to be a heritage maker. You have something worth passing on, and you are called to do just that.

INDOCTRINATION

I have a few heirlooms that may seem trivial to other people but which are priceless to me, precious remembrances passed from generation to generation. One such remembrance is a leaded glass bowl that Sherri's great-aunt gave her. Something in the way it was passed from hand to hand, the way our great-aunt's fingers traced its pattern caressingly one last time, a reluctance to let it go, that tenderness told us of the bowl's value. I learned two things from this rite of receiving: (1) We appreciated its value not only for its intrinsic worth but because of the tender affection our great-aunt lavished upon it, and (2) a good deal of the giver came with the gift. Our most significant bequests to our children are those spiritual legacies, those relationships, those heaven-given heirlooms that we treasure.

The Bible tells us that if our faith is vital, we must consciously pass it on. We will handle it with caressing hands. Grateful hearts will repeat cherished stories of God's faithfulness and sustenance. Tears will speak of the preciousness of our salvation. Loving prayers will plead for our children's salvation and heritage in the Lord. We will pass the treasure along.

Notice again the urgency of this sentence from Deuteronomy: "Impress [God's commandments] on your children." The word *impress* literally means to stamp the commandments of God onto your children's minds and hearts. Oh, if it were only that easy! If only each morning we could again parade our children past us and with holy ink stamp the message of Christ anew upon them. Sounds silly doesn't it? That's why I read with interest what James Dobson says about the imprinting of a tiny gosling.

Q. "Should a child be allowed to 'decide for himself' on matters related to his concept of God? Aren't we forcing our religion down his throat when we tell him what he must believe?"

A. Let me answer that question with an illustration from nature. A little gosling (baby goose) has a peculiar characteristic that is relevant at this point. Shortly after he hatches from his shell he will become attached, or "imprinted" to the first thing that he sees moving near him. . . . Ordinarily, he becomes imprinted to the mother goose . . . however the gosling will settle for any mobile substitute . . . [even a football]. The gosling is vulnerable to imprinting for only a few seconds . . . if that opportunity is lost, it cannot be regained later.

There is also a critical period when certain kinds of instruction are possible in the life of the child. Although humans have no instincts (only drives, reflexes, urges, etc.), there is a brief period during childhood when youngsters are vulnerable to religious training. . . . As in the case of the gosling, the opportunity of that period must be seized when it is available. . . . The absence or misapplication of instruction through that prime-time period may place a severe limitation on the depth of the child's later devotion to God. When parents say they are going to withhold indoctrination from their small child, allowing him to "decide for himself" they are almost guaranteeing that he will "decide" in the negative. . . . The child listens closely to discover just how much his parent believes what he is preaching; any indecision or ethical confusion from the parent is likely to be magnified in the child.*

Do you understand what Dobson says? Essentially, he affirms that we *do* stamp our faith (be it Christian or humanistic) upon our children. This stamping is not accomplished in a moment but in the way we live our lives as they observe those lives during the years of their development. Call it indoctrination or whatever you like. Our faith affects our children's faith. I find an interesting parallel in Scripture to what Dr. Dobson says.

*From: *Dr. Dobson Answers Your Questions*
By: Dr. James Dobson © 1982
Used by permission of Tyndale House Publishers, Inc.
All rights reserved.

46

Joshua 24:16-18 records the pledge that Israelite parents made to serve God faithfully: " 'Far be it from us to forsake the LORD to serve other gods! It was the LORD our God himself who brought us and our fathers up out of Egypt . . . and performed those great signs before our eyes. . . . We too will serve the LORD because he is our God.' "

These parents had seen what God had done. Not only that, they knew God himself. One would think that after a pledge like that their children would be assured a place in the heavenly realms. That kind of commitment on the part of parents makes one anxious to read about the children. Well, we get the chance to do just that in the book of Judges.

Note this from Judges 2:10: "After that whole generation [those who had made the pledge reported by Joshua in the passage quoted above] had been gathered to their fathers, another generation grew up, who knew neither the LORD nor what he had done for Israel."

What happened? Where was the slipup? Somehow the parents failed to keep their promise to pass on to their children an account of God's faithfulness and of the promise they'd made to be faithful to him. The Israelites failed to imprint the facts and their faith upon their children's hearts. Somewhere between head and heart a generation was lost. The parents made their pledge with passion, but somehow mothers and fathers failed to impress the stamp of God on their children's lives. Why didn't the children know what God had done for Israel? The offspring never experienced the heritage of saving faith lived out in their presence. Perhaps the greatest tragedy of this failure was that faith was so near, in their hearts, and slipped so far. We have the opportunity to pass along a heritage to our children, and then the privilege of watching them surpass us in faithfulness if we will only impress gospel truth upon them.

The natural question is this: How do I ensure that I will be able to stamp them indelibly with this gospel ink? Deuteronomy tells us. "Talk about [God's commandments] when you sit at home and when you walk along the road, when you lie down and when you get up" (6:7).

INTEGRATION

When Pat and Jill Williams visited Francis Schaeffer, he told them he had based his life on biblical principles. One principle concerned prayer

47

and the family. He urged them, "Commit your family to a life of prayer." Consequently, the Williamses advise, "There should be daily prayer, individually and together, committing everything to God and trusting Him to meet even the smallest needs. Such a discipline undoubtedly led to [Schaeffer's] own natural way of praying anywhere, any time, and you can be sure that it rubbed off on his children."[4]

I want to be known by my children as a man who wore his faith in a very visible manner.

In college, I took a class that was designed to help us integrate our faith and learning. Later when I became a teacher for a time, I looked often at the notes that I had taken in that class. I wanted to rediscover that specific way in which to teach my students so that they could see that God is active in history. It did not occur to me until after several years of teaching that they did not so much need to see God in history as they needed to see God in me. Integration of faith and learning then became a natural by-product of my teaching. Vital, living faith just cannot be hidden. If you in fact have such a faith (rather, if faith has you), not only are your conversations peppered with references to faith and to your relationship to Christ, your life attests the genuineness of that of which your mouth speaks.

If I am asked where I integrate my faith into rearing and training my family I must answer, "When I sit down and when I rise up." Christianity is not a religion; it is a relationship, and that relationship permeates every aspect of my life.

Talking to and about God with our children is second nature, so much so that we may even be unconscious of the habit until someone points it out to us. That is what happened to a dear friend of mine. She relates this touching story of a child's desire to pray.

She had invited to lunch some of her children's friends who did not have a heritage of faith in their family. The host family, however, paused just before mealtime each day, bowed their heads, and prayed. It was a natural part of the family life and of the parents' love for God, but totally foreign to the visitors, especially one small boy. Convinced that these people knew something he did not, he screwed up his nerve to ask for instruction.

"Mrs. Farlow, will you teach me how to read my plate like you do at mealtime?"

She was puzzled by his request.

He explained, "Well, before every meal you read your plate. There's nothing on my plate. I want to read my plate to God like you do."

Analyze your conversations as well as your lifestyle and your home. How obvious is your faith? What will be written of your children's generation? Will they know what God has done in your life, and, more important, will they know God for themselves so that they can pass the heritage on to their children?

It was John who wrote the words that would be, to me, the most significant epitaph for my tombstone: "I have no greater joy than to hear that my children are walking in the truth" (3 John 4).

A prayer for parents:

They are asleep, O God, and I am so very tired, but before I go to sleep begin tonight to make me all that I want them to become.

AN EXERCISE IN PHILIPPIANS 2:12b–13

1. Not everyone is a storyteller, but all of us can tell stories. Think of two or three instances in your family life that bore the signature of God. Perhaps the birth of a child or getting your job. Maybe it's the story of your conversion. Now find a chair large enough for two and tell the story of faith and God to your child. Children especially love stories in which they are a part.
2. Imagine an account of what excuses Israelite parents might have had concerning reasons for their not passing their faith along to their children.
3. Recall an important "imprinting" moment in your faith pilgrimage and thank God for that special event.

4
Building Their Faith

The following brief story appeared in *Reader's Digest*. Even though this is only an excerpt, its likeness to real life is striking.

> "I'm Reid. I do the trees," he said. "I'll be back in a few days."
>
> When Mr. Reid returned, I began to learn what it meant to "do" the trees. He sprayed twice more as summer progressed, and as the apples matured, he thinned them.
>
> Mr. Reid "did" our trees for the next twelve years. But he did far more. My children became his devoted helpers, and he taught them many things—about trees and the birds and the insects, but also about work and self-respect, dignity and trust. . . . Bits of his wisdom became their wisdom—and mine.
>
> "Mr. Reid says a tree gives back something for everything you do for it," my younger son remarked one evening as we sat before a blazing fire. "He says we must never waste anything a tree gives us."
>
> I could hear him saying it. Something in the way he said "tree." The way he ran his hand along a branch, was close to reverence.
>
> "You do trees the same way you raise youngsters," he said one day when I commented on the care with which he chiseled away an awkward knot so the bark could grow across the wound. "You can't protect them from the elements, but you can understand what they're up against and guide them so they'll bend and not break."[1]

Bending not breaking. Here is the essence of parental concern and our heart's desire.

What loving parent does not look at their children and pray that they will never be subjected to a life that would break them? It is an innate desire to protect them from disappointment and disillusionment. Yet I have always been in awe at how close to the breaking point prayer takes us. Prayer makes us vulnerable.

In counseling, I often ask a married couple each to tell me what his or her spouse's dreams are—not what their goals are, but their dreams. The "if I could do anything, be anything, accomplish anything" dreams we all have tucked nicely away in safekeeping in our minds. I have found that people will reveal those dreams only to one whom they really trust. "I trust you with this dream. I trust you will not laugh when I express it, that you won't dash it, that you won't tell it to others, but that you will honor it." As they respond to my question, they often reach out for each other's hand as if to say, "Don't worry, you can still trust me with this dream. I will not hurt you or belittle you."

In a very real sense, prayer is sharing our dreams with God. It opens us up, and makes us vulnerable before God. We come to him, trusting that he will not snicker at our request or dash it against the rocks. We ask that he honor this dream we reveal. But we put ourselves at risk in the process. We realize that we are absolutely dependent upon him for fulfillment of those desires of the heart.

Close friends of ours visited our house and upon their return home found that their cat was missing. Well, you can imagine the rest of the story. Their children wanted to pray for that cat—earnestly pray. Not for one day or two, but they pledged to pray until that cat came home.

What do you do in a situation like that? Do you tell the kids that in all likelihood Honey is dead? Do you say that the odds of finding a lost cat are one in 756,000? Do you drive around throughout the night calling out in hushed tones, "Here, Kitty, Kitty," hoping all the time not to wake the neighbors but somehow to get the cat's attention? Do you visit your local pet store to see whether they have a cat that looks exactly like Honey, then try to pass him off as the real thing? As a parent, you may be willing to do any or all of these.

Listening to my children's prayers can sometimes be the most difficult part of teaching them to pray. I have a tendency to protect them from any kind of disappointment or disillusionment. When I hear a prayer from their lips, framed in such innocence, my heart compels me to intervene in any way—to orchestrate its answer—to spring into action. *But then, who becomes my children's God?*

To pray is to move beyond our own resources and trust God. Prayer is faith in action. And so my children joined their friends in praying for the safe return of Honey the cat.

She showed up at our place nine days later. Apparently she had hitched a ride under the hood of their car near the motor where she could keep warm. Safe and sound, the cat was returned to the arms of two young children whose faith grew through their willingness openly to place their faith in God. Someone has said that you can measure your faith by what you dare publicly to affirm. When it comes to publicly affirming faith, children display nothing less than holy boldness.

Faith is built by baby steps. While I try to resist the temptation to orchestrate answers to my children's prayers, I want to help them pray so as to build their faith. Out of this incident with Honey, three simple principles popped into my mind to help build children's faith through prayers. First, parents should guide their children's prayers. Second, parents must be convinced of the power of prayer. And last, parents must learn to let God be God. By that I mean, leave the results of our children's prayers with Him. We don't have to defend God when our children's prayers are not answered as they had hoped. However, we should explain that God has something better waiting for them.

52

GUIDING CHILDREN'S PRAYERS

As a boy, I recall coming to my father for money to buy a set of walkie-talkies. It did not seem like an extravagant request, but at the same time, I knew our family was short on money. My father explained to me that there simply was nothing in the budget for walkie-talkies, and I began to move away dejectedly when my father made a simple suggestion. His idea opened up a whole new world to me.

"Let's pray about the walkie-talkies, Keith."

We had never prayed about something like this, so I asked him for an explanation.

"Why don't we ask God for a way to get those walkie-talkies?" Dad suggested.

I don't know exactly what Dad had in mind, but I began praying that evening, and the next evening, and the next evening, and the next

evening. It was not very long until I received a phone call from the newspaper delivery coordinator in our area. He asked whether I wanted to earn some spending money working as a newspaper delivery boy.

With my first paycheck from that job, I gave a tithe and bought a set of walkie-talkies with the rest of it.

I don't know how you might feel about that essentially selfish prayer, but in that moment I realized God had answered my prayer. That answer to prayer shaped my life. That little nudge toward prayer opened the door to "faith-full" prayer in my life—not just for myself but in intercessory prayer as well.

When we think about teaching our children to pray, we must guide their prayers. When a child has reached the age where he is petitioning God, it is time to help direct his requests. It is truly cruel to let a child's faith be dashed because we didn't take the time to help him understand God's directions for proper prayer.

Matthew 7:7-11 will help a child to understand prayer:

> "Ask and it will be given to you; seek and you will find; knock and the door will be opened to you. For everyone who asks receives; he who seeks finds; and to him who knocks, the door will be opened.
>
> "Which of you, if his son asks for bread, will give him a stone? Or if he asks for a fish, will give him a snake? If you, then, though you are evil, know how to give good gifts to your children, how much more will your Father in heaven give good gifts to those who ask him!"

From this passage of Scripture, I want my children to understand four things about prayer. These are simple concepts that do not need to be taught all at once, but that do need to be taught nonetheless.

1. *God wants us to pray, and he tells us to ask.* God has established prayer in such a way that he responds to our asking. The epistle of James tells us that God cannot, or at least will not or does not, respond to our silence. The apostle writes, "You do not have, because you do not ask God" (4:2). I have met adults who do not want to pray for their businesses or their jobs or their personal needs. They are afraid that petitions of that nature will sound selfish to God. God wants us to ask and has commanded us to ask. You must test your motives (v. 3), but we are everywhere invited and urged to ask. We must encourage our children to ask.

2. *God tells us to seek*. Seeking is earnest appeal to God. Seeking lets a child understand that prayer is not a flippant wish list for Father Santa. James 1:6 says of the person who prays, ". . . when he asks, he must believe and not doubt, because he who doubts is like a wave of the sea, blown and tossed by the wind." To pray without faith in God makes the petitioner like an ocean wave, here one moment but receding into the sea the next. Our seeking must be earnest. To bring this truth down to a child's level, explain that earnest seeking is just the way the child searches for a very favorite toy that he or she has misplaced. The seeking continues until the toy is found. We pray in the same manner. (I've spent half my parental life looking for pacifiers, and any parent will understand me when I say that I search *very, very* earnestly for it until I find it!)

God must be especially concerned to establish young believers' feeble steps of faith. By the same token, prayers that are tossed to heaven as if they really aren't all that important to the pray-er will undoubtedly receive no divine response.

3. *Knocking opens the door to God*. The idea of knocking helps children understand that they are taking their requests to a very important person—God himself. You never barge through a door without first knocking, especially on a person who deserves our respect. More important, though it establishes that we are not there to demand of God, knocking denotes a certain recognition of sovereignty. I knock before entering my daughter's room. She is sovereign in that room. God is *God*, and we approach him in honor. He has said that we may bring requests to him. Knocking emphasizes the etiquette with which we approach God.

Children seem to comprehend this so much better than adults at times. Children are used to authority in their lives. They have no right to demand anything of their parents. They must ask. The command to knock, which at the same time is an invitation, gives us opportunity to show God in the same light—the light of honor.

We can help guide our children's prayers by explaining to them the importance of prayer on these three levels: asking, seeking, knocking. Are they asking flippantly? Are their requests concerns that are here today and gone tomorrow? Are they earnest about their prayers? Are their prayers selfish? These simple questions and simple insights can help children determine for themselves the right way to pray. In addition, this affords us a perfect opportunity to explain the fourth principle.

4. *God is a loving Father and loving Friend*. He will give us only what is truly best for us. This concept properly conveyed allows us the opportunity to say that if our loving Friend knows that something will not be good for us, he will not give it to us. Children are not shocked when God says no. Parents must often say no to their children. If, as parents, we have taken time to explain our negative responses our children will begin to understand that some of their requests are not best for them. There will be times when as parents we say no and when God says no. They will learn to submit to God just as James tells us to do.

God does not withhold his love or favor. Nor out of cruelty does he withhold answers to our requests. He is interested in us with unconditional love, love that never intends to hurt. The fact is that we live in a fallen and imperfect world. Even adults sometimes look upon God as some sort of heavenly vending machine. I tell my children that as often as possible I will say yes. In fact, we have made this a point in our lives. Too often we say no without even considering the request. God, too, says yes whenever it is possible. Because of that, when we ask, seek, and knock, we know that God is giving to us his very best.

BELIEVING IT WITH ALL YOUR HEART

I heard a story of a small town in which there were no liquor stores. Eventually, a night club was put up on Main Street. Church members in the area were so disturbed by the club's presence that they planned all-night prayer vigils. They protested to the Lord about this den of iniquity. A short time later lightning struck the tavern, completely destroying it.

The next day the owner of the tavern sued the church for damages. His attorney claimed that their prayers had caused the loss. The congregation on the other hand hired a lawyer to fight the case saying that they had nothing to do with it. After much deliberation the judge ruled: "It is the opinion of this court that, wherever the guilt may lie, the tavern keeper is the one who believes in prayer while the church does not."

Humorous, isn't it? We profess belief in the power of prayer when it accords with our needs and wishes, but our true convictions often are that

56

prayer is impractical in the real world and that *we'd* better get to work if we genuinely want something to happen.

My daughter and I were sitting in our run-down car at the drive-up window of our local bank. (My wife refers to that jalopy as my mobile eyesore.) As I put the car in gear to leave, the motor hiccuped and stalled. I had to push it out of the drive-up passage where I popped the hood switch. Peering at the engine, I tinkered for a moment as though I knew what I was doing. I shook, I bumped, I pleaded, and then I jumped back into the car and twisted the key. Nothing. Twice, three times, four times. Five times I went through the ritual and still nothing.

Finally, Whit said, "Daddy, I think we had better pray that the car starts or we're going to be stuck here."

Now, I wish I could tell you that I did the spiritual thing. I wish that I could tell you I took my daughter's hand and said, "Let's pause for prayer right now, Whitney." I wish I could tell you that I seized this moment to rise to full spiritual-giant stature and teach her that Daddy prays for everything and trusts God for everything. I wish, I wish, I wish I could tell you that. But I didn't.

"Right, Whitney, you pray real quick, and Daddy's going to try the car one more time."

I jumped out and headed for the hood again. After three more efforts, I looked over at my daughter's face. The look told me something was wrong.

"What's up, Whit?" I asked.

"Well, I guess God just isn't listening to me."

Tell me what would go through your mind at that moment? Spiritually I felt two feet tall.

"Yes, God is listening, but I think God wants us to have some time for a Coke and a talk."

I took her hand, and we walked across the street to a fast-food restaurant and grabbed a Coke. Then we walked the two miles home—a little girl on her daddy's shoulders—talking about how God listens to our prayers.

"Whit, God always listens to us when we pray, and God always cares."

57

I wasn't afraid to admit, "Daddy doesn't always understand when God acts and when he doesn't. But I know this, Whit. I trust him."

I rediscovered a bit of childlike faith that day. I wouldn't trade that hour with my daughter for a new car!

I was told once that kids don't give us opportunity to prepare for exams. Children give only pop quizzes. I had my pop quiz. I failed it, but I am not about to blow the makeup exam!

I have to admit that often the faith I display to my children is a diluted faith due to lack of earnestness. If we are to teach our children how to pray, we must be thoroughly convinced of the importance of prayer in our own lives. This conviction applies not only to the importance of prayer, but also to its power.

Kneeling at her bedside one evening, my daughter and I prayed for three children. She wanted to pray for their salvation. (I'll have more to say about this later.) We prayed for the children in turn; she prayed first and I followed. I prayed like this: "Dear Jesus, I pray that somehow you might let Casie, Kevin, and Carl start coming to church and . . . "

Whit interrupted me, exclaiming, "*Might* come to church? Dad, you mean *will* come to church, don't you?"

My daughter had caught the suggestion of unbelief—the question mark that I left for my way out in case the prayer was not answered. The Lord reminded us that faith as a grain of mustard seed is all it takes to move mountains, to call upon his power. This means no hesitant "might" or "but"; we are to call with faith upon God's power.

Most of us have learned ways to couch our prayers in phrases that are innocuous enough so that we don't lose face if the answers we seek are not granted *as* we wanted. That kind of praying results in an attitude that any answer is acceptable regardless of what it is. *That practice is to pray without power*. We have a form of godliness, but we deny the power thereof (2 Timothy 3:5). We have learned not to risk too much or be too vulnerable in our prayers. We guard ourselves very carefully by the terms we use. This unhappy and ineffectual practice is not what I mean by guiding children so that they will bend but not break. Quite the contrary. If we neuter our prayers, our children are certain to be broken in the future by God's lack of action and by their lack of ability to pray with force and effect. If we are to teach our children to pray, it must be with hearts believing.

Take a moment, even now, to examine your heart and your prayers to see whether you pray in such a way as to "hedge your bets." Do you pray in faith believing? If you need help in this matter, no book will revolutionize your prayer life more than Wesley Duewel's *Mighty Prevailing Prayer*.[2] He skillfully describes the power that is available to us through believing prayer.

LET GOD BE GOD

A fat cat lazily lounges on the back of the couch. He is called the "prayer cat." This cat is the possession of a dear mentoring family in my spiritual life. They tell his story with a smirk. It seems that their daughter began to pray that somehow God would soften her papa's heart, allowing her to get a kitten—a heart not easily softened to a cat. It would have been easy for her mother to manipulate the answer to that prayer, perhaps slipping a note to Papa or telling him after the children had gone to bed. It would have been even somewhat excusable to let Papa know that much of their daughter's faith was riding on this prayer cat. That was not the mother's way. She and her daughter prayed and prayed; and they prayed that God would soften Papa's heart so that they might have a kitten and that Papa would even learn to love it. The cat lazes atop the sofa with an "attitude" as his story is told. Its presence is testimony to God's power to change a heart in what we might consider a trivial matter but that to a little girl was a faith-building experience.

I mentioned earlier that it is our parental tendency to want to orchestrate answers to our children's prayers. We meddle wherever we can so that their disappointments are few. Yet again, in meddling we only set them up for future crushing disappointments and disillusionment. If we are truly to teach our children to bend and not break, then we must also let them learn to let God be God.

Some people would advise us that if we tell our children God can do anything, we become Satan's agents in destroying their faith. To such an unbiblical assertion, I respond that we must teach our children of God's awesome power and his sovereign rule. Some say this is too difficult for a child. I don't think so.

Perhaps nothing is more disappointing to a child than to pray for a little lost dog or cat and to learn that his pet has died or run away and will never come home. It hurts us as mothers and fathers to watch their shattered dreams and their little card houses collapse upon them. At the same time, possibly the most precious way we can participate in these prayers is to enter into the children's grief that results from prayers not being answered as they had hoped. There are times when life kicks prayer right out of us, even when we are children.

Maybe, as a parent, this is the time to tell your sons and daughters the story of a difficult prayer that you once prayed only to have God say no. You will want to add how God gave you grace and how you learned to believe and trust God through that disappointment and how you can now see that it all was for the best. That is when God makes us to be encouragers to our children.

I recall a seminary friend telling of his daughter who was lying in bed during an unusually violent thunderstorm. She called out to her daddy to come help her. He came into the room, but, as seminary dads are apt to do, he saw this as a wonderful teaching opportunity. He knelt beside her and explained that she did not need to be afraid because Jesus was with her and Jesus wouldn't leave her. The little girl responded, "I know, Daddy, but right now I need something with skin on it."

There are times when God calls us to be skin-bearing encouragers, someone, when disappointments loom large, who has been there.

I can't always protect my children from what they are up against. But I hope that through guiding their prayers, believing in prayer, and letting God be God, I can help them to bend and not break.

AN EXERCISE IN PHILIPPIANS 2:12b–13

1. Recall your own jalopy story in which a child's faith and faithfulness outshone your own.
2. It would be tragic if you were unprepared for the time your young disciple needs a skin-bearing encourager. Think about one of your disappointments in which you experienced God's grace and victory.
3. Listen to your prayers. Identify any escape clauses. Reach for God's power.

5
Making Prayer Understandable Without Making It Trite

Kids are bound to get some things mixed up. It seems that they are always twisting a phrase or jerking things out of perspective. A condensation of Judith Frost Stark's *Priceless Proverbs* appeared in *Reader's Digest* in 1985. Judith gave her class of six-year-olds part of an ageless proverb and asked them to complete the saying. Here are the definitions the children came up with when left to their own imaginations.

"A miss is as good as a . . . mister."

"Laugh, and the world laughs with you, cry and you . . . have to blow your nose."

"A penny saved is . . . not much."

"He who marries for money . . . better be nice to his wife."

"It is always darkest before . . . daylight savings time."

"When the blind leadeth the blind . . . get out of thayr way."[1]

Kids need to put things in kids' language, so they reduce things to words and phrases they understand. You've doubtless heard of the children who were heard singing, "While shepherds washed their socks by night"! Or the Sunday school boy who sang, "Bringing in the sheep."

These are not intentionally humorous. They simply reflect children's ways of trying to make sense out of the adult world they live in. It must be very difficult. So how much of prayer do they comprehend? Well, it is obvious from listening to children pray that they understand a great deal. Still, so much must go right by them that we have to take care to present prayer on a child's level.

In prayer we need to be age-sensitive. Certain words do not communicate to children. They come upon concepts and learning at different stages through different ages. Sometimes we make these stages too restrictive as if God were not able to give them insights beyond their years. Jesus lifted his face heavenward on a day and exclaimed, " 'I praise you, Father, Lord of heaven and earth, because you have hidden [spiritual truths] from the wise and learned, and revealed them to little children' " (Matthew 11:25). God has used children to communicate concepts well beyond their years, but for the most part we tend to hold children captive to general developmental guidelines. This unfortunately has tempted some to reduce prayer to childishness. Take care not to make prayer trite—or to trivialize God. I am not a fan of those who want to refer to their heavenly Father as their "Daddy" in heaven.

Here are two principles to keep in mind to help us communicate effectively with our children: (1) Avoid speaking "Christianese" and (2) use language appropriate for their age and level of maturity.

AVOIDING CHRISTIANESE

Because I deal with many people whom I want to see come into a personal relationship with Christ, I try to be conscious of the terminology I use in conversations. At first, I could not believe how difficult it was to eliminate evangelical jargon from my speech patterns. Someone has said that within two years after a person becomes a Christian he can no longer communicate effectively with non-Christian friends. I've been a Christian from age eight and was brought up in the church. I was a jargon junkie. I knew all the terminology and their definitions and could rattle them off with ease, but my friends had no idea what I was talking about. "Grace" is unmerited favor, "justification" is just as if I never sinned, and "righteousness" is right before God. And so forth. "Eutychus," a columnist in *Christianity Today*, took our lingo to its logical extreme in this humorous little excerpt:

> . . . my church has given me the assignment of helping our new members learn Christian jargon. After all, they have to be able to communicate at coffee hour.
>
> . . . I began with a discussion of such basic terms as the "old nature" and the "new nature." When I asked for definitions, a class

wag immediately said, "Old nature is last year's leaves and new nature is this year's leaves."

It was down hill from there. I asked for a definition of "justification" and someone shot back, "what you need when under stress (just a vacation)." I said "sanctification" and someone replied, "what happened to the boat on vacation." I mentioned "denying yourself" and somebody cried, "the process of removing one's 'ny' "! I muttered "discipleship" and someone said "a fishing boat belonging to Peter."[2]

The unfortunate thing of this humorous article is its truth! From words like, "lift them up" and "glorify" and "admonish" to "sharing," "exhorting," and "ministering," we have our own language. The list goes on *ad infinitum*.

I wish that an admonition to stop using Christian jargon were sufficient to bring its use to a halt, but the fact is that most of us don't realize what we sound like. Then we hear our children parroting phrases that they probably do not understand.

One young convert stood to testify before her baptism. "I was the most wretched of sinners before Jesus found me and pulled me from the mire." She was only eight years old! Now, I know that sin is sin, but just how *wretched* are most of the eight-year-olds you know? And where did she get the word *mire*? Is there really any question?

So how do we know which words *do* communicate and which *are* appropriate when talking with children?

Listen!

That's right, listen so that you can use their vocabulary. If a spiritual idea can't be expressed in their words, then it is probably too advanced for their present state of spiritual maturity. If, in the language of five-year-olds, we can't tell five-year-olds what confession of sin is, we must wait—wait until we have discovered phrases in their language that will help us explain what we mean.

In talking with children, let's jettison our theological language and substitute nickel words for it all. I'm not saying that there are not times and places where use of technical theological terminology is appropriate. But I am saying that those times and places are fewer than we usually suppose.

My daughter never said that God was omnipresent, just that he was everywhere. She didn't need to use the word *omniscient* to say that God knows everything. She has never "lifted someone up before the Lord" nor has she asked for God's "blessing upon this person." But she has said, "I really want you to help them, God."

God doesn't become less than God when addressed in simple speech; he becomes more comprehensible.

UNDERSTANDING AGES AND STAGES

While it is important to adjust our language, we should also have some acquaintance with characteristics of children at the various social/emotional/spiritual developmental stages. Although some draw the lines on development too strictly, it is wise to know the general guidelines so that we are not expecting more than our children are capable of delivering.

Possibly the best way to get at this is to put this information into a few simple charts.[3] (This material is adapted from *Gospel Light's Teaching Tips*.) Any division will be artificial to some extent and restrictive. I have broken these out into three age groupings, using broad brush strokes for easier viewing of the stages of social/mental/emotional/spiritual maturation.

Ages 2 and 3

Social Development
>   Seeks personal and physical contact
>   Anger and similar emotions lie near the surface
>   Moods changeable
>   Plays alone and in groups
>   Sees self as the center of universe
>   Relevance found only in immediate concerns
>   Lacks language skills to communicate effectively, frustrated by limitations

Mental/Emotional Development
Concrete and sensory, learns and categorizes information through senses
Communicates in word pictures
Loves repetition
Explores and experiments

Spiritual Development
Interested in God
Understands that God loves him/her
Understands that God takes care of him/her
Understands that God wants to hear about him/her
Understands that Jesus is his/her Friend
Open to explanations of ways God helps with anger, fear, anxiety

In this stage of development children will respond to questions, but they are not able to make logical connections. One young boy made this clear in a grocery store. Lost, he wandered until one of the clerks saw his forlorn look and took him to the front desk where the manager took him by the hand and began the search for his mother. At the head of each aisle, the manager asked, "Do you see your mother?" And at each aisle the boy replied, "No." They covered the entire store in this fashion, aisle after aisle. Becoming concerned, the manager took the child to the front of the store and stood him on the counter. "Look over the whole store. Do you see your mother?"

The little boy responded, "Nope! I just keep seeing my dad"!

Bible stories are so vivid for a child of this age because they are visually concrete to the child. Prayer may still be difficult to comprehend even though they love to participate. They have no way to understand God except through you. Your touch, your love, your acceptance are all equated with God's. There is no more vulnerable stage of spiritual development! This is the gosling stage of which Dobson spoke. Pray while holding them close. Let them "feel" prayer as much as hear it.

66

Ages 4, 5, and 6

Social Development
      Wants adult approval
      Responds to friendliness and love
      Interested in social friendships
      Plays well with one other playmate, usually excludes a third
      Makes pretending a major pastime
      Is easily embarrassed

Mental/Emotional Development
      Makes tentative assertions of right and wrong
      Questions to gather facts
      Begins to deal with abstract concepts

Spiritual Development
      World concern has expanded
      Wants to know that God loves all people
      Relates to God through other adults
      Might pray on by self about personal concerns
      Needs specific examples of how God works and is active
      Understanding of Pretend helps comprehension of God as nonphysical
      No longer satisfied with simple spiritual equations; desires to know how it all fits

Four- and five-year-olds suddenly begin to see deficiencies in their parents' spiritual lives and holes in their explanations of spiritual truth. One little boy was comforted to hear that his grandmother, who had died, would be in heaven with God forever, but when told that his dead cat would be there too, he asked, "What is God going to do with a dead cat?"

This is a precious time of spiritual development, and some at this age may even come to believe in Jesus as Savior. (We will speak of that in the chapter on salvation.) This is the age to stop limiting talk about God to Bible stories and begin to show how God is at work in everyday life. It is also a time to teach biblical principles of right and wrong, stressing obedience as relationship, not law.

Ages 7 to 9

Social Development
>   The age of teasing, nicknames, and criticisms
>   Self-identity based on peer recognition
>   Makes deliberate and deliberated decisions on right and wrong
>   Decreased dependence on adults
>   Looks to other adults for role models

Mental/Emotional Development
>   Given to bragging and "one-upmanship"
>   Loves to play with language
>   Applies logic to life situations

Spiritual Development
>   Open to reinforcement of Jesus as Friend
>   Begins to sense need for God in different situations
>   Open to hearing about need for salvation
>   Understands the concept of God's forgiveness

In reality, pinning down the development of a child is like sticking gelatin to a wall. This is especially true as children grow older and their characters become more complex. The point can still be made, however, that we must teach our children to pray in ways that are understandable to them. Anything short of this makes prayer seem like a grown-up thing to do and robs them of that precious relationship with a loving heavenly Father.

Many books have been written by experts on stages in childhood development. You will want to seek additional reading by consulting the following.

>   James Dobson, *Dare To Discipline*, Tyndale
>   James Dobson, *Dr. Dobson Answers Your Questions*, Tyndale
>   James Dobson, *Hide or Seek*, Revell
>   James Dobson, *The Strong-Willed Child*, Tyndale
>   Wes Haystead, *Teaching Children About God*, Regal
>   Jay Kesler, ed., *Parents and Children*, Victor

John Trent and Gary Smalley, *The Blessing: Giving and Gaining Family Approval*, Nelson
Pat Williams and Jill Williams, *Keep the Fire Glowing: How a Loving Marriage Builds a Loving Family*, Revell

6
Prayer of Salvation

Crowds always press upon him, touching, talking, some even taunting. But today is different. Jesus is seated as he teaches. The conversation is for adults. The talk is of divorce—its historical, theological, and personal implications. Suddenly children appear. Of all places for them to be, why here? Why now? It is hardly appropriate. So the disciples' rebuke of the insensitive parents who brought them is quite in order. This is, very simply, not the right moment for children to be blessed by Jesus.

So haggling begins between the Twelve and the sets of parents concerning the appropriate times to bring children to Jesus. Historically it is seen as inappropriate because of the topic and the teacher. A child cannot possibly comprehend what it means to be blessed by Jesus. A child cannot understand who this great teacher is or all the implications of his coming. And they certainly don't need to hear this argument over a correct theological understanding of divorce. Yes, rebuke is in order for those who would think of bringing a child to this One, this Jesus—the Messiah, the Savior.

But then we read this loveliest of Jesus' invitations: " 'Let the little children come to me, and do not hinder them, for the kingdom of God belongs to such as these' . . . And [Jesus] took the children in his arms, put his hands on them and blessed them" (Mark 10:14–16).

I am thankful that as an eight-year-old boy I was not met by a rebuking disciple but by a loving parent when I asked to meet Jesus. I knelt and earnestly asked him to be my Savior. The greatest miracle of the universe happened at that moment as God entered my life. Thank God the kingdom of heaven is made up of ones "such as these."

CAN A CHILD BE SAVED?

Touching on the issue of childhood conversions can be risky business indeed. It is a topic certain to ruffle feathers on every side of the issue. If you tell a parent whose four-year-old has just prayed a precious prayer for salvation that a child of that age cannot possibly understand what he or she did, you will undoubtedly be faced with an incredulous parent. And you may do well to escape with all of your body parts intact.

Or, on the other hand, if you speak to those who are familiar with theories of childhood development and how children come to faith, you may meet arguments based upon Piaget's sensorimotor stage and the preoperational stage, and how children cannot conceptualize, integrate, and accept an infinite being. Or your antagonists may bring up Fowler's "Stages of Faith"[1] and his concept of intuitive-projective faith, along with the mythical-literal model. They may want to argue theological and biblical concepts such as culpability and original sin as if an intellectual understanding of soteriology were necessary before one can actually experience salvation in any meaningful way. (This is not in any way meant to denigrate the importance of adults spending their entire lifetime as students of God's Word and of theology. Christians should be the very best informed believers they can be. No Christian is excused from loving God with his or her mind.)

I wrote the above with tongue in cheek. Spare your friends and save the technical jargon for the technicians.

I am a pragmatist. That means that I am concerned with theory only as it coincides with reality. If anyone can walk the line on this issue of a child's salvation it is the pragmatist. The pragmatist is not concerned with parents or practitioners. The only pertinent question is "Does it happen?"

If my children tell me they would like to be a part of Jesus' family, I would not load them down with a response like, "I'm sorry, but you will have to wait until you understand the dualistic nature of our world and the existential nature of the soul." I would want to say, "I'm so excited for you. Once Daddy did the very same thing, and it has made all the difference in his life. Let's talk about it."

I will admit that communicating the essence of salvation to a child on a child's level is difficult. Most of us have witnessed programs where a well-meaning individual has urged children to salvation and the whole group has gone forward. Wes Haystead writes:

> The fact that a young child is easily manipulated . . . complicates the issue. He succumbs to the right kind of pressure. Most young children keenly desire to please the significant adults in their lives. They endure innumerable inconveniences to earn a smile, a pat, or a word of commendation. Recognition from adults is one of the strongest motivators in the young child's experience. The parent or teacher who asks the child, "Would you like to ask Jesus to forgive your sins?" is more likely to have the child respond out of a desire to cooperate than from a true conviction or understanding of what is happening.[2]

He is right, you know. But how different are adults? Many of us have seen altars lined with people because no one wanted to appear to be the only one not responding to the masterfully manipulated call. No one wants to be the only one left standing in the pew on the last verse of "Just As I Am," especially when the preacher announces that one more person needs to respond. But in this type of situation where does the fault really lie? Isn't it in the communicator rather than with the receptor? When one sees evangelism of children done by those gifted in communicating truths on a child's level, many of the issues of the theorists are erased.

SALVATION WHERE KIDS CAN REACH IT

Myron and Julie Stump have a ministry of evangelism of children. I know them, and I know their faith, but as a skeptic and standing behind the children, I watch critically and observe how they work their love through the group of youngsters.

From the back of the room a UPS man enters riding his bike and honking his horn. Once, twice around the sanctuary. (I'm certain this is a first in this church.)

"Special delivery!" he shouts.

Julie responds, "A present for me! Oh, thank you. Where do I sign?"

"No, no, no! This is for *God*, and it is from *Jesus*. Jesus paid for it, and he wants the children here at Kids' Connection to see it first," says Myron, the UPS man.

Julie reads the tag.

"This gift is for God from Jesus. This gift is irreplaceable. Nothing can take its place. It was specially chosen. It is unique in every way— very, very special! It is lovable and huggable and already assembled . . . and it even has movable parts."

"Wow! It's full of energy and needs no batteries because it is plugged right into the power source. But this gift is also very fragile and must be handled with care. I wonder what it could be?

"It says it is a reflection of the Creator and that a very big price was paid for the gift."[3]

By this time my skepticism is fading along with the children's, and I am as excited as they are when Julie offers to unwrap the gift. But now she stops.

She turns to one of the children and asks her to unwrap it instead while Julie holds it precisely and the girl unwraps the present.

The squeal tells me it is something special, but then the exclamation drives the message home. "It's me!" the child cries as she gazes into the mirror Julie holds. Helpers distribute tiny mirrors to every child. On the mirror is printed, "I'm special." The children who can't read are told what it says. You would think they had never seen their reflections before. They are delighted to know that they are special gifts from Jesus to God.

As parents arrive to collect their children, each young person shouts, "See, I'm special."

In increments, Julie and Myron lead the children to understand the concepts of salvation concretely. This is merely one example of dozens they use. Four days of these types of presentations prepare children to understand what it means to know and be part of God's family. When "altar calls" are made, avalanches of children do not come forward— instead a few thoughtful decisions each evening are made, and seldom does a child come twice.

It seems that salvation, when presented to a child, related to the child's needs, and on a child's level becomes understandable and accessible even to them. Yes, they do not fully comprehend. Who of us does? But in talking with these children I am amazed at just how much they do understand.

On the grounds that we may leave essential elements out of the salvation message, some may take exception to our relating the message to children's needs or on their level. If by "essential elements" is meant that the children may not be told about hell and eternal punishment or that substitutionary atonement may not be explained, the exception-takers are correct. This is where the salvation of a child may be different from that of an adult.

SALVATION: POINT AND PROCESS

Some speak of salvation as a process that one grows into. There is not, they say, a day when one is not saved and then a day when one is. Rather, as one becomes more and more aware of God, one simply accepts "salvation" bit by bit. One *grows* into a state of salvation.

I cannot accept this. Salvation is always a point-time event. I mean by that phrase that a moment in time comes when one makes a *decision*. If one cannot make a decision, then one cannot be and is not saved. This is clear from Scripture. However, a child's salvation decision may differ from an adult's. The most important distinction is the information and understanding on which the decision is based.

That is, children may realize first that Jesus is a special friend with whom they can talk about anything, or they may learn first to appreciate his love about which they have been told. Children may decide on the basis of this information alone that they want Jesus to be their friend. This is good, but, scripturally, it does not constitute salvation. It does however open the door for parents, pastors, and teachers to begin to talk with children about *salvation*. It is the first approach of that grace that leads to salvation as it enables children to sense a need, the attractiveness of our Lord, and an intuitive awareness that they and Jesus were made for each other.

Wes Haystead paints a possible scenario that conveys what might be going on in a child's mind.

> Five-year-old Jason's father was very pleased when his son announced, "Daddy, I want Jesus to come into my heart."

He responded by saying, "I'm very happy that you are thinking about this, Jason, because it is the most important decision you will ever make in your life. Tell me, what do you like most about Jesus?"

This question was less threatening than a straight, "Why do you want to become a Christian?" and thus was easier for Jason to answer. Also, his father hoped it would reveal some of Jason's thoughts and emotions about the Lord.

"I guess I like the way He fed all those people with the boy's lunch," was Jason's reply.

"That was one way He showed people that He loved them," said Dad. "Tell me some other things you like about Him."

Jason mentioned several other events from the life of Jesus, and finally mentioned that he liked Jesus because He loved everybody.

"That's a good answer, Jason. I love Jesus very much, because I know that He loves me."

"I love Jesus, too," said Jason.

"Let's tell Jesus that we love Him."

Following very simple prayers by father and son, Dad asked, "Jason, do you want to talk about this some more right now, or do you want to do it tonight at bedtime?" Jason had had enough for one session, and ran outside. As Dad thought about their conversation, he noted that Jason had not expressed any awareness of how Jesus related personally to him, other than that He loved him.

That night, Dad asked Jason, "Do you remember what we said about Jesus this afternoon? Do you want to talk about Him some more?" Jason did. Then Dad said, "We talked today about loving Jesus. Tell me what people do when they love someone very much."

Jason thought. "They do kind things. They want to make them happy."

"That's right, Jason, Now tell me what happens if someone does something to a person they love that makes them unhappy."

"You have to say you're sorry," was Jason's reply.

"Tell me what it means to be sorry," Dad continued.

"Sorry means you are sad you did something, and won't do it again," Jason said.

Dad looked straight into Jason's eyes. "Now I'm going to ask you a hard question. Have you ever done anything that made Jesus unhappy?"

This question led Jason to confession of several acts that he felt were wrong. It was an easy step here to lead Jason to a prayer in which he said he was sorry for what he had done wrong.

"Jason, Jesus loves you very much, even when you do something bad. But, I am sure He is very happy because you have told Him you are sorry for those things. Let's talk about this again in a few days."*

In Haystead's scenario, conversations between dad and son continue over a period of time, and he writes that it is a memorable day when Jason specifically asks Jesus to forgive him for his sin and became a member of God's family. But it certainly was not during the first time father and son had prayed about such things.

In the scenario, when did this young child come to the point of salvation? I don't know. I can't tell whether it was when he realized wrong and said he was sorry or when he finally connected all the pieces and asked specifically to be a part of God's family. Distinctions at this point can be blurred. This is what I do know: that child made a decision sufficient for salvation. The building blocks had been laid consistently for the child to understand and to pray (ask) for salvation.

I have also noticed something else about salvation of children. They may have understood the Gospel only in part, but they continue to increase that understanding of their salvation as parents, teachers, and pastors support their decision in conversation and in prayer time.

I will often sit with my daughter, Whitney, and ask her to tell me about the day she asked Jesus into her heart. I've noticed that as she has learned more about God and her relationship with Jesus, the story has expanded to include new details. A child's salvation, like an adult's, is both point-time and process. It is process in that continual growth in comprehension and reaffirmation is a part of a relationship with God. It is growth also in loving God until we reach Jesus' goal for us: " 'Love the Lord your God with all your heart and with all your soul and with all your mind' " (Matthew 22:37; see Deuteronomy 6:5). As Whitney (or any other

*Teaching Your Child About God by Wes Haystead
Copyright 1983
Regal Books, Ventura, CA 93003
Used by permission

child) learns more about God, she draws this love and grace and understanding into her salvation story.

With that in mind, I must say that the most crucial element of a child's commitment to Christ is not the decision taken by itself but the discipleship—the talk and rehearsal of the decision and its meaning. It is, after all, God's goal to create a people for himself, and that people is created by growth in likeness to Jesus Christ our Lord. One afternoon I was trailing my son on his bike when he began to ask questions about God. Eventually, he expressed a desire to tell God he was sorry. But the story really only *began* there because he continues to learn how to appropriate that experience into his life.

Did you notice that word *discipleship* pop up again? I know it is overused. It is one of those buzz words to which we have become desensitized, and so we have quit listening. Realistically, children have only a sliver of a chance if we talk with them about the plan of salvation and then leave it at that. Our children's faith can take root only if we do the following:

- Listen to our children

- Repeatedly ask open-ended questions to probe and challenge their minds

- Allow concepts to come when they are developmentally ready

- Stand prepared to enhance those concepts with concrete applications to their Christian lives

We reinforce this "growth in grace" as we support the principles with reference to relevant biblical material.

Whitney and Keaton were sitting on our laps while my wife, Sherri, and I read from a children's story Bible. The lesson for that evening concerned Joseph and his brothers. At the conclusion of the story, we took a few minutes to let our budding young actors portray the characters. (No Academy Awards were presented for this, but sometimes they come up with some heartrending interpretations of biblical truth. At other times it is purely heretical; er! I mean hysterical.)

When we finished I thought of Genesis 50:20 and quoted it to Whitney. As Joseph looked back on his brothers' treatment of him when

78

he was only seventeen, he made a timelessly relevant observation: " 'You intended to harm me, but God intended it for good to accomplish what is now being done, the saving of many lives.' " I saw Whit thinking, so I waited for her to talk. Pretty soon she asked, "Do you mean God can take even bad things and make them turn out to be good?" My daughter had just paraphrased Romans 8:28 (". . . we know that in all things God works for the good of those who love him"), and she had grown a little in her comprehension of God. We took time to relate to Whitney specific stories of how God had turned bad into good in our lives as well. It was a wonderful learning time. I think this is a portion of what Paul meant when he said, ". . . continue to work out your salvation with fear and trembling, for it is God who works in you to will and to act according to his good purpose" (Philippians 2:12b–13).

I am not foolhardy enough to assert that a child can comprehend the Gospel in all of its intricacies. But God can teach us something new about himself whenever we apply ourselves to his Word. The words are still true. The Gospel pond is deep enough for an elephant to swim and shallow enough for an infant to wade.

At our church one Sunday morning, someone overheard a conversation among three children. One said, "They said this is God's house."

"It's big enough for God," said another.

A third, posing the more rational question, asked, "If this is God's house, I wonder how he got in here."

The first child was not to be stumped. "Because someone gave him a key to get in," he replied.

Unwittingly, that child may have stated more about salvation than he knew. Perhaps, though, he stated what we need to do. We need to help our children find Jesus as their personal Savior by giving them some keys—one at a time and step by step.

Can a child accept Jesus as a personal Savior? We must answer that affirmatively in every sense of the word. Jesus illustrated the truth of it when he told us to become as little children in regard to our faith and trust in God.

If you are looking for that miracle formula for salvation or the soothing balm of a guaranteed commitment to our Lord by your children, you have been desperately disappointed in these pages. But I hope, if you are looking for the opportunity to open the door for your children to understand and accept salvation, that you may have been encouraged along the way. Regardless, I beg you to give your children the keys so that they can hand them to Jesus and let him into their hearts.

AN EXERCISE IN PHILIPPIANS 2:12b–13

1. Your children are apt to give a pop quiz when it comes to asking you about salvation. Out of the blue they may ask questions. You can't wait till that moment to "get ready" to explain God's plan. Jot down three open-ended questions that might help them understand their present relationship to Jesus and the relationship that He desires for them. Use Mr. Haystead's piece to help you. That is, "Tell me what you love about Jesus."

2. If your children have already accepted Jesus, work on reviewing that decision. Listen for new understandings on their part. Listen also for a grasping of these essentials:
   - "I'm sorry" (forgiveness)
   - "God loves me" (acceptance)
   - "I love God/Jesus" (personal response)
   - Concrete applications to life of this new relationship (behavior, daily time for Bible reading and prayer)

3. Describe for your children the specifics of your becoming a part of God's family.

7
Prayer Etiquette

Have you ever been to one of those formal affairs where it is necessary to think back to your training in etiquette to recall proper form and behavior? Which fork do you use for this part of the meal? Why is the knife at the top of the plate? Who should be seated first? How does one make a proper introduction? It is enough to give you an ulcer.

These kinds of functions can be exhausting, but everyday life presents its own etiquette agony. The evidence of this can be found even in our popular magazines. Each month Elizabeth L. Post offers authoritative answers to urgent questions in *Good Housekeeping*, questions from people like you and me who find themselves on the horns of the etiquette dilemma. You know, essential issues like the following:

> My daughter wants to invite to her fifth birthday party all the children in our immediate neighborhood except one little boy whom she detests. I understand her wishes (the boy *is* a bully), but I don't want to hurt the boy's feelings or offend his mother. What should I do?
>
> I invited five couples to dinner but didn't ask if they had any food allergies or particular dislikes. My friend says a good hostess always does that. Is she right?
>
> I often jog outside my office complex at lunchtime. Am I being unforgivably rude if I don't answer drivers who call out to me to ask directions? By stopping, I sacrifice attaining my aerobic heart rate.[1]

How would we get along in life without knowing the correct response?

Etiquette is one of those essentials in life. Even though some take it

82

to extremes, as in the situations above, proper etiquette is something that caring parents instill into their children.

What does etiquette have in common with teaching children to pray? A good deal more than one might expect. Etiquette is a learned response. We learn acceptable behavior through exposure to new social situations and through repeated exhortation. My mother told me at least twice to get my elbows off the table and to stop slouching. (You straightened up when you read that, didn't you? It is a conditioned response. See how well you were taught!) What surprises me is the number of areas where basic rules of etiquette apply in our approach to God in prayer.

I mentioned in the introduction that we should not allow prayer to degenerate into the flippant rehearsal of any and every thought. That kind of restraint is a form of prayer etiquette. Through prayer I introduce my children to the most precious relationship of their lives, to *God*. That is awesome indeed. While I will not let approach to God become legalistic or ritualistic, I want my children to approach him with honor, to know that God is majesty and to be highly esteemed. These are adult ideas, to be sure, but applicable to children, too, if they are presented correctly. This is where simple etiquette comes in. The common courtesies that we show to one another should also be observed in our relationship with God:

Be considerate of others' needs and share what you have.

Ask politely and say please.

Don't be demanding.

Say thank you.

Apologize when you have hurt someone.

Saying "I love you" is a special gift you can always give.

Treat others with kindness.

We can easily dovetail our lessons of common courtesy with lessons about our relationship with God in prayer if we simply use some creativity. The Bible is full of stories that illustrate both interpersonal and faith etiquette.

Sherri and I like to teach these concepts through stories that we then act out. Any number of other creative approaches can be used to reinforce the concept. For example, Luke 9:46–48 is only one biblical passage that parallels the courtesy we want to show God in our prayer relationship:

Be considerate of others. In this brief paragraph from Luke, we come upon an argument among the twelve disciples about who is the greatest of them. This issue seems especially appropriate for children because if there is one argument I have heard time and time again, it is the one over who has the best doll, the best dad, the best school, the worst cold, the greatest sadness, and so on. You name it, kids want to be the top of the heap regardless of the nature of the heap. (Wait a minute! It's not only the kids, is it?) I remember as a child sizing up other men to see whether my dad could beat them up. Can you imagine what would have happened if I had ever issued a challenge on behalf of my father? This passage clearly tells children as well as adults how we are to see and conduct ourselves— and it is not as "the greatest."

Let the story guide you as you teach etiquette, but do not be afraid to take little stories from your children's lives and make the application. Luke 10:25–37 has the story of the Good Samaritan with its sound principle of obligation to those who need help. In addition to reading Bible stories, we use the "McGee and Me" video series and the Odyssey series put out by Focus on the Family and Tyndale House as a visual aid to discussion.

Ask politely and say please. Matthew 15:21–28 speaks of a woman who, although a Canaanite, comes to Jesus for the healing of her daughter. Her persistence and faith allow her to receive from the Lord her daughter's healing. We can use this story and others like it to illustrate God's willingness to help those who have faith, have great need, and are willing to ask.

Don't be demanding. The story of the centurion's request in Luke 7:1–10 shows how even a man of great honor made humble requests of Jesus. This story affords a great learning opportunity in the proper approach to God.

Say thank you. The story of the healing of the ten lepers (Luke 17:11–19) could not be a more vivid account of God's desire for us to cultivate gratitude of the heart. The response of simple thankfulness from one of the lepers warms the heart of Jesus while the lack of response from the other nine sends a chill through the spirit.

Apologize when you have hurt someone. I enjoy telling the full story of Jacob and Esau (Genesis 32:1–21; 33:1–15). As Jacob comes across the desert he expects nothing but murderous hatred from his brother. His peace offerings can be seen as feeble attempts at saying he is sorry. Children like this story because sometimes saying "I'm sorry" is difficult for them. The story also opens an important issue that is often neglected in praying with children—the need to tell God that we are sorry. Nothing is more humbling than seeking forgiveness. Even young children realize this when you direct them to ask forgiveness of a friend or sibling. If we neglect confession, we rob our children of the relief and sweet release from God for sins committed.

We choose bedtime in our home as a time of reflection as well as relaxation. At times I must ask my children's forgiveness and my heavenly Father's forgiveness. This is painful, this confessing that I have sinned against my children and against my God. But to receive forgiveness from each has been sheer delight. This experience is reinforced in *Building Your Family to Last*:

> . . . I used to sit at the bedside of my children and give them time to review the day's events. Sins were often confessed. I confessed, and they confessed. Those were very holy moments of the day when the slate was wiped clean between us and our God and between each other.[2]

Proper approach to God is just another tool for us to use as we teach our children more about their relationship with God. Your own creative imagination will help you apply with original flare the principles of this chapter. Don't adopt wholesale the methods our family has taken. Each family is different, and prescriptive formulas only leave families of differing styles feeling uneasy. Use your own methodology and enjoy your own family. Still, it is easy to see the value of prayer etiquette, which acts as a safeguard to flippant familiarity with God. Respect for God is something I come back to as often as I recall my mother's warnings about elbows on the table and slouching. The latter has allowed me to function with society; the former has given me a wonderful relationship with God.

85

AN EXERCISE IN PHILIPPIANS 2:12b–13

1. Use each of the following stories and create your own "etiquette" principle:

- Rich Young Ruler (Matthew 19:16–22)
- Jonah and the Great Fish (Jonah 1:1–17)
- Peter's Denial (Luke 22:54–62)
- Naaman (2 Kings 5:1–14)

2. Think of three ways you could make a Bible lesson come to life through drama, art, song, etc.
3. In what ways might a person display "flippant familiarity" in prayer?

8
Letting Them Touch Their World

Before you read this chapter, I need to give you a peek into the Wooden homestead. Otherwise, you might read this and think we live in some kind of commune.

The Wooden home is an open home. I mean that God allows us to share our home with a variety of guests. It is not a large house by some standards, but we have found that friends are not looking for large houses; they are looking for loving homes. We live a very transparent existence. Dirty laundry, misbehaved children, and family disagreements are all open to view. But so is support, love, and friendship. We took our cue from Karen Burton Mains's *Open Heart—Open Home*.[1] We have never regretted our transparent living. God has given us so many precious relationships through it.

In our six years in this house, God has brought all types of people to share our home. Our prayer has been "that God will bring the people of His choice to us, and keep all others away."[2] In response to that prayer God has sent folks from nearly every walk of life. Several have come from the gay community to our door looking for help. Battered wives and their children have lived with us until able to reestablish themselves. In addition, marriage partners catapulted toward divorce have lived here. All have shared our family life on equal footing with our family.

God sent a Japanese girl named Miho, who called this place home for a season; and a missionary lived with us for a precious year. Evangelists and pastor interns have found respite and refreshment.

I did not fully realize how transient our new friends are and how full our home usually is until my daughter, whose job it is to set the table, began to ask, "Dad, how many people are going to eat with us tonight?"

Hardly a weekend goes by that new folks have not put their feet under our table or otherwise tucked themselves into the shelter of our home. I truly thank God for that.

That said, let me begin to tell you about how children touch their world through prayer with an account of possibly the most tender moment our family has witnessed.

A young man, an alcoholic and a drug addict, had come to stay with us for a few weeks while he was waiting to get into a "detox" center. Longer-term guests had already staked their claims to the bedrooms. He was living in our living room on the sofa bed. He had no privacy because our children rise early, and the living room is their primary turf.

My son became attached to Jeff in just a few short days. One evening we sat down to dinner together, and Keaton asked to pray. As he prayed, he began his custom of praying his way around the table. He got to Jeff and thanked the Lord for letting Jeff stay with us. I know you are supposed to have your eyes closed in prayer, but I was looking. I looked at Jeff, and he was crying!

My two-and-a-half-year-old son had just touched the heart of an addict through prayer.

I cried too!

I have watched and listened as my children have effectively touched their worlds through prayer. We sell our children short when we limit their prayer concerns or trivialize the answers that come to their prayers.

It pained me to read one writer's suggestion on teaching children to touch their world. She recommended the following:

Almost daily we use our cars; while on longer trips, ask God to protect certain people you pass on the road. Take turns deciding for whom you will pray. Because you can't specifically pray for every traveller, you might limit prayer to those driving red Volkswagens, semi-trailers, or out-of-state cars. Be as general or specific as you wish.

"Lord, protect that lady in the VW. Bring some Christian into her life who will tell her You love her."[3]

As cute as this may seem, it trivializes an area of prayer that we want to cultivate in our children. It is sometimes easy to love the whole world and pray for everyone when we are praying for no one specifically. I want to let my children know specifically (1) what they are praying for, (2) whom they are praying for, and (3) when those answers to prayer arrive. This is the only way to teach children the dynamic and powerful resource we possess in intercessory prayer. Anonymous riders in Volkswagens will remain anonymous, and my children will never realize how they affect the lives of others if they follow this plan.

I want to tell you of the time when our children prayed, and we saw God's most powerful miracle—the changing of a human heart.

Our family practices lifestyle evangelism in every facet of life. It is our passion to see individuals come to know Jesus as their personal Savior. To us that means inconveniencing ourselves in any fashion for the sake of the Gospel. My wife and I make it a policy to identify five people within our circle of friends to whom we are consciously trying to build bridges for opportunities to witness.

I usually schedule at least one lunch a week with a non-Christian. Over the course of several years, we have seen several of our friends come to the Lord in this manner, and God has dramatically changed many lives.

We recently chose for a prayer target a man named Alan and his wife, Carrie. They are valued friends to us indeed, and we have begun our friendship on several different levels of common interest. We will build any bridge we can without compromising our Lord. Along with these contacts, we made it a regular practice to pray for Alan and Carrie every night. To let our children know how important Alan and Carrie are to us, we include the children in this praying. We recognized the couple's importance to us when Whit and Keaton began to pray for them as well.

Too many Christians associate only with other Christians. But how are we to introduce people to the kingdom of God if we work and play only with our own kind? The day came when Alan and Carrie invited us to a birthday party at their home. We knew that alcohol would be served and some would be smoking. Still, we like this couple and wanted not only to develop the friendship but also to bring them into a saving relationship with God. Sensitive to the fact that the presence of liquor and tobacco would be a problem for our children, we explained that in order for Alan and Carrie to come to know Jesus, somebody who loves Jesus needs to be a part of their lives. We reassured them that we do not drink or smoke and that we wouldn't be influenced to take up those habits. But, we told them, we want to be with Alan and Carrie so that we might someday have a chance to tell them about Jesus. The kids seemed to grasp our point, but I didn't realize how much they had understood until a few days later when my wife was praying with Whitney.

"Mommy, who can I be praying for like you pray for Alan and Carrie?"

She wanted to pray for someone's salvation like Mommy and Daddy did. We asked her to think of someone she knows who doesn't know Jesus. I am amazed at how perceptive children are to their friends' spiritual condition. It goes way beyond just observing whether they go to church. God gives children a discerning heart also. She had no difficulty coming up with three friends who didn't know Jesus. She wanted to pray for Casie, Kevin, and Carl. And so we began to pray not only for Alan and Carrie, but for Whitney's friends.

Each night we prayed that the three would (not "might," mind you) come to church. Not only that, but that they would one day accept Jesus Christ as their personal Savior. We prayed thus for several weeks, in faith believing that somehow through Whitney's life, Casie, Kevin, and Carl would be touched.

One night Whitney came home from a children's crusade that was then in progress at our church. The leaders asked the children to invite their friends so they could hear about Jesus.

Whom do you think Whitney wanted to invite?

Our five-year-old called Casie, Kevin, and Carl and invited them to go with her the next night. At the end of that meeting, eleven-year-old Casie committed her life to Christ. It was a beautiful decision. Casie was the first to answer the invitation to know Jesus as her Savior.

Whitney returned from that crusade on cloud nine. She was so excited. The amazing part was that though she had received the award for bringing the most friends, to her that was not point. Her greatest reward was seeing a friend for whom she had prayed come to know Jesus.

Do know that a child can affect his or her world!

90

That evening our daughter had a taste of what it is like to touch the world through Jesus Christ. She realized the power of prayer in Casie's life, and it has intensified her prayer for other children who do not know Jesus Christ.

Children touch their world as they understand it and at the level they experience it. If we teach them that prayer is intangible, they will perceive it that way and practice it that way. This assessment of how children can pray brings us to simple steps to follow in our teaching them how to touch their world through prayer.

OPEN UP THEIR WORLD

A child's world is only as large as the experiences to which he has been exposed. Here we Christians have many advantages, if we will capitalize on them.

We can avail ourselves of the world that comes to the door of the church. If your church is a missions-oriented church, invite missionaries to stay in your home while they minister in your church. Whether it is for dinner, overnight, or an entire furlough, the result for your children will be greatly to extend their hearts and minds to new horizons.

One family in our church has hung a world map on the living room wall. On the map are the locations of the missionaries they support and their pictures. The children in this family have opportunity literally to pray around the world for people whom they know personally because when the missionaries are home, they often visit here. I appreciate a family that will sacrifice a little decor for the impact an emphasis on spirituality can have on their children.

When I was a child, a family down the street had a special bedroom set aside for visiting missionaries. It is amazing how much that concept affected my thinking, but I am even more amazed at how it influenced their children. Each of their children is now in full-time ministry for the Lord.

Here is another idea for school-age children. Have them select classmates for whom they will pray weekly. Don't simply scan the list of names or the pictures of the children. Encourage your children to pinpoint specific needs their friends have. Perhaps one of the children is going

through the pain of parents' divorce. Or perhaps another child's grades are poor. This has a double effect. It allows your children to pray specifically for other children, but it increases awareness of children outside their circle of friends.

I wouldn't be true to myself if I did not also put in a plug for touching your neighbors and friends. If your children hear you praying for the salvation and other needs of those who live near you, they will begin to understand the lostness of their friends and relatives also.

One family's prayer for a father's salvation illustrates just how much children understand about salvation and eternity.

Sarah (six) and Hannah (four) prayed nightly for their daddy to want Jesus in his heart. When he did accept Jesus their prayer was moving.

"Thank you, Jesus, that all of us will get to be with you and Daddy forever and that Daddy won't have to be alone."

It is no understatement to say that children will not touch their world until the world has touched them. It is a risky proposition to let the world touch our children, but I recall what Christ said of his disciples: " 'My prayer is not that you take them out of the world but that you protect them from the evil one' " (John 17:15).

The world is so vast and the needs are so great, but we touch it in prayer one person at a time. You will listen with awe as your children reach around the world or across the street through prayer, and you will know that your heavenly Father is hearing and acting on their words.

The ancient Greeks had a special athletic event called the torch race. Each contestant was expected not only to finish the course but also to reach the end with the torch still aflame.

Rearing children is not only a task to complete, but a spiritual mission of great consequence. The task of equipping our children with the ability to touch the world through prayer is not an option for Christian parents; it is the flame.

AN EXERCISE IN PHILIPPIANS 2:12b–13

1. For whose salvation are you faithfully praying? Do your children know about it?

2. In what areas do you water down prayer through generalizations in prayer rather than making specific requests?
3. List several ways in which you can expand your children's world through exposing them to more of its realities.

9
Praying for Your Child

My son was eight days old when my wife resumed her concert ministry. He traveled with her because she was nursing him. Near the end of the concert Sherri borrowed a song from Wayne Watson and on the stage she sang it to Keaton, whom she held in her arms.

These are the words to the song she sang:

> *Somewhere in the world today,*
> > *A little girl will go out to play*
> *All dressed up in Mama's clothes,*
> > *At least that's the way I suppose it goes.*
>
> *Somewhere in the world tonight,*
> > *Before she reaches to turn out the light,*
> *She'll be praying from a tender heart,*
> > *A simple prayer that's a work of art.*
>
> *And I don't even know her name,*
> > *But I'm praying for her just the same*
> *That the Lord will write His name upon her heart.*
> > *'Cause somewhere in the course of this life,*
> *A little boy will need a godly wife,*
> > *So hold onto Jesus, baby, wherever you are.*
>
> *Somewhere in the world out there,*
> > *That little girl is learning how to care.*
> *She's picking up her mama's charms,*
> > *Or maybe swinging 'round in her daddy's arms.*
>
> *Somewhere in the world to be,*
> > *Though the future's not real clear to me,*

Theirs could be a tender love,
Grounded in eternal love above.

And I don't even know her name,
But I'm praying for her just the same
That the Lord will write His name upon her heart.
'Cause somewhere in the course of this life,
My little boy will need a godly wife,
So hold onto Jesus, baby, wherever you are.[1]

She sang the song—correct that—she sang as much of it as any mother could expect to sing while holding her newborn son and thinking of his future.

This song is certain to produce a tear whenever it is heard. Can a Christian parent not be deeply touched through its message? The idea staggers my mind that a girl is out there, growing up for my son to marry; and that somewhere in the world a little boy is growing up who will become husband to my girl. What's more, the thought that I can pray for those children and their parents boggles my mind even more. But I agree—"Somewhere in the course of this life my son *will* need a godly wife." Wayne Watson has a way of pulling the eternal values out of the mundane and putting them to beautiful music. This song appeals to my sentimental nature, but how does it fit with reality?

I must admit it did not square very much with my reality until recently.

A few years ago my father accompanied me on a job interview to northern Michigan. Dad came along to help make the long overnight return trip. (I do some of my best sleeping at the wheel, so I try not to drive much at night.) The night before the interview we were lying in our beds when Dad began to pray. It was just like days gone by—Dad praying, me listening in. But this prayer was different from the prayers of my youth. This had an added dimension.

My father prayed for my children and their future mates. That might not have been so strange if I had had children. But I didn't. In fact, children were not even a glimmer in my eye and would not be for two years. But there was Dad praying for them just the same, as if they were there. Nameless, nonexistent children brought to our Father in prayer for

96

their life and relationships. How odd! Praying and planning my children's future even before their conception!

But suppose we could write the blueprints for our children's lives. What a wonderful idea! I mean, if we could plan out the days for them, it would eliminate a lot of worry.

Think how you would map out your children's future. Plan the occasion of their first steps. Determine their first words. Take them safely through their first day of school and make sure no big kid spoils their lives by making fun of them. Figure out what you will say when your daughter tells you she is not a little girl anymore. Make sure you are ready when your son gets in his first fight. Think about how they will respond to adolescence, dating, drugs, and how the two of you will get along through all of this. Plan their lives and their relationships so that no harm will come their way and they will be spared life's traumas and hurts. Write the script so that they live happily ever after. Don't miss a thing. Be sure to dot every *i* and cross every *t*. Then once you have finished, sit back and relax. The next ten, twelve, or fourteen years will be a breeze. Why not? You have it all programmed. Right?

Now take a reality pill! Perfect children are not a part of our fallen world, not even yours. Not even though you've prearranged everything.

This is reality: No matter how much I would like to be able to script my children's lives, they will be played out in the uncertain world of reality. And reality is tough! At best, we have only limited influence on our children. Beyond the reach of our embrace they are left to live on their own. Although we will pour every human resource into them and saturate them with love, we have only one way really to affect our children for good—that way is prayer.

Even the thought of my children approaching school age sends shivers up and down my spine. It makes Mark Twain's advice on children seem reasonable and sane.

"When a child turns thirteen, put him in a barrel and feed him through the hole; when he turns sixteen, plug up the hole."

I long for quick fixes, but there are none when it comes to rearing children. That project can never be reduced to an event. It will be a forever process—a never-ending concern as every parent of adult children will attest. In the pagan society we've created for ourselves, we are going to have to pray for our Christian children, if they are to make it through safely and triumphantly!

THE RHYTHM OF LIFE

Whether we like it or not, life has its own rhythm, a rhythm that we cannot so much choose as one with which we will be forced to get in step. Life marches to the cadence of time and season, as summed up for us in Ecclesiastes (3:1–2, RSV; emphasis mine).

For everything there is a season, and a time for every matter under heaven:

a time to be born, and a time to die;
a time to plant, and a time to pluck up what is planted.

Within those seasons and times, the cadences and meter that we march to, we face a rhythm in relationship to our children. When we pray for them, we must be ready for two things: (1) We must give them to God, and (2) we must have the courage to take them back again.

The best way to illustrate what I'm saying is to let you see the movements play themselves out.

GIVE THEM TO GOD

I reached out and touched the shoulder of a woman who had just lost her ten-year-old son in a freak accident. I felt her grief, shared her tears, and realized her sense of irretrievable loss. I wanted to say I understood, but I didn't—I couldn't. The truth is, I really didn't want to be able to say I understood. I couldn't honestly say that I would want to share her path. Even looking at her from the comfort and security of my own life made me sense my own vulnerability, and I wanted to retreat to the safety of my own world. I drove home and walked into my son's room. He was sleeping, and I took him in my arms and held him. This was my life. This was my world, and it was still unscathed. I prayed selfishly but earnestly, "God, please don't ever let him go. Let him stay forever. He's so tender, God, please don't ever let him go!"

I held on tight, thinking that my clutching would secure God's promise.

As I held him, thoughts came to me of a story I have been told repeatedly throughout my life:

"When you were eighteen months old, Keith, we nearly lost you."

It's a story that as a child I loved to hear my mother tell. She told it as no one else could. She always left me with a sense of special identity—as if God himself had taken care of me for a very special reason.

"You were days away from gangrene. Your body so dehydrated we laid wet washcloths on you to keep you moist. We kept thinking you had the flu—so did the doctors—but the condition persisted. Finally, we had to admit you to the hospital. It was only with the surgeon's insistence that our doctor told us exploratory surgery was the only chance for your survival. You suffered from Incidus Invertus—a fancy way of saying you were put together backward inside. You were so close to death. They had your tiny arms tied down so you wouldn't pull out the IVs. When we came to see you, you cried and hugged us with your legs and feet."

When death visits your child that closely, you talk with God. My parents prayed and bargained and prayed again for my survival. The fact that I am here certifies that their prayers were answered, but in the process Mom and Dad grappled with the possibility of having to let me go.

Later when my parents dedicated me to God, their pastor read, " 'I prayed for this child, and the LORD has granted me what I asked of him. So now I give him to the LORD. For his whole life he will be given over to the LORD' " (1 Samuel 1:27–28).

My mother knew what her pastor was asking when he said, "Would you give your son, Mrs. Wooden?"

Hadn't she already dealt with this question once? Did she really have to answer again? God had already brought her to the point where she had to grapple with the possibility of the death of her son, and now the pastor was asking her to give him up again. To be honest, Mom says she was looking for an exit from the church and an escape from

that question. She didn't know whether she was prepared to make that commitment again.

Finally, tearfully, she said, "Yes, I will give my son."

Symbolically, the pastor took me from her arms and gave me again to God.

No matter how tightly I hugged Keaton I realized he could still slip right through my fingers. Maybe it would not be in death, but life could steal him from me just as readily. Releasing my grip, I also gave in to God. I let go of what I really never possessed.

"God, I can't hold him tight enough. You hold him!"

The most pertinent question I could ask you right now is this: Whose really are your children? Have you ever given them to God in prayer? We can't begin to pray for our children until we have entrusted them to God's care. If we are still clinging to them with a tenacious grip, we have never really trusted God for their well-being. Earlier I mentioned that praying is often like telling God your dreams and trusting for their outcome. Praying for your children is like taking your dreams to God and completely letting go. But to what degree can we claim ownership anyway? The mother crying over the loss of her son told me clearly that the ways and welfare and times of our children are in the hands of Another.

"God, I can't hold him tight enough. You hold him!"

Can you pray that way? Will you stop now and make Hannah's prayer your prayer for your children? " 'I prayed for this child, and the LORD has granted me what I asked of him. So now I give him to the LORD. For his whole life he will be given over to the LORD.' "

She looks down at her angel
  Sleeping in his bed.
She gently kneels beside him;
  Then she bows her head.
Just like other mothers
  Who lived so long ago,
She brings her child to Jesus
  And gives him to the Lord . . .

. . . .

101

"Jesus, here's another child to hold;
Keep this child safe and warm
['Cause] this world can be so cold.
Take this child in your arms
And never let [him] go.
Jesus, here's another child;
Jesus, here's a precious child;
Jesus, here's another child to hold."[2]

HAVE THE COURAGE TO TAKE THEM BACK

Giving our children to God is only half of the equation, however.

Thirteen years were to pass before my brother and father would play out another part of this rhythm of life.

It was in the late sixties/early seventies. Times were changing, and a generation was waiting for no one. My father and my brother stood toe to toe on the slate entryway of our home. Though I could hear only snatches of their conversation, the harshness in their voices came through clearly enough and told me more than I wanted to know. "You will not use drugs while you live in this house—not with your brother and sister still here." My brother tossed back some of the thinking of the sixties and seventies, the rejection of traditional values that swept the country. Then I heard my father say, "I think it's time for you to go, Son." My brother walked out of the house and my father cried. With wings big enough to flap but not strong enough to bear him, Tom flew away from home, from father, from mother, from me.

Was Dad giving up on my brother? Was he washing his hands of his son? Not at all! Dad regarded Tom's departure as a summons for him to pray even more fervently. Long since, my parents had given Tom to the Lord just as Hannah had done with Samuel. When we realize that those we give to God *are* God's—that he loves them and cares for them and that we are only stewards entrusted with them for a time—we will stop clinging to them, and we will rededicate ourselves to fervent prayer to the One who cares for them the most—their heavenly Father. This is what I mean by "taking them back," taking them back to give them to God all over again.

Confused and rebellious, Tom left home and took off across the United States, heading for California. He was, he felt, at last out of my parents' grasp. But I recall their prayers for him—begging God with tears to take care of their dear son and to bring him to salvation.

Their arms were too short to reach Tom, to embrace him. But God's were not. A month after he left, he found himself in Las Vegas. He was empty—spiritually, morally, emotionally, physically. And his gas tank was empty, too. Like the Prodigal Son of Luke 15, Tom was on the verge of coming "to his senses" (v. 17). He pulled into one of those all-night wedding chapels and fell at the altar to pray. (This had to be a first in the history of that little chapel!) A man alone at the altar with only God there with him. What a sight! The bewildered attendant didn't have any idea of how much to charge him for the time he stayed at the place of prayer.

God touched Tom's heart three-quarters of the way across the country. While this child was well beyond the guidance of mother and father, he was still within touch through prayer.

The greatest freedom in the world has to be the freedom we experience in praying for a child who has been dedicated and given to God. We are not praying in generalities. We are not pleading for the Lord to intervene. We are talking about our children to the One who loves them most of all and who desires much more keenly than we ever could that they find themselves through finding him.

Prayer power comes when we are willing to let go of our children and then take them back to God in continuing prayer—to give them up as a possession and take them back as a trust! Hold them close and then let them go.

How simple it is to pray for our children when they are faced with difficulties or when we are faced with their crises, but how wonderful just to pray for them, for their todays and their tomorrows. Donald Gray Barnhouse was once asked about the proper time to begin to influence children concerning their relationship to the Lord. He answered wisely, "Twenty years before they are born."

Will you pray now, giving your children to God? And then will you take them back as a trust from God, accepting your responsibility to rear them and nurture them in the fear of the Lord? Do so at once.

103

TEACHING CHILDREN TO PRAY

Parents' Prayer:

Father, I thank you for these precious gifts of my children. I want to acknowledge that they are yours and that you have entrusted them to me for only a short while. Teach me to hold them close, to let them go, and to pray for them.

AN EXERCISE IN PHILIPPIANS 2:12b–13

1. Have you intentionally given your children to God? How did it affect you?
2. Perhaps you have a wayward child. If so, take time to read *The Hurting Parent* by Margie M. Lewis and Gregg Lewis, mother and son (Zondervan).
3. To stress the importance of Christian mates for our children and of God's provision, we pray each night with them for the ones whom they will marry. We have explained that not everyone marries but that those who do must be aware of God's rule: Christians are not to marry unbelievers (2 Corinthians 6:14).

Afterword

I have read many books that gave "how-to" instructions, only to find myself frustrated. Things never worked out quite the way the designers said they would. Not even my Nestlé Toll House cookies turn out the way other people's do. How-to formulas, especially when applied to the dynamics of people, inevitably leave one feeling like a failure. Meanwhile, that family in the book you just read sounds so perfect. How can your family ever measure up? Well, relax. This only proves one thing, authors have erasers and notoriously short memories. Your family, your children, your life situation all require that you "feel" your way through life. If you want to call it rearing children by the seat of your pants, well, I guess that is what it is to some degree.

I have not intended in this book to draw conclusions for you or to give you pat answers. My desire has been that you come to your own conclusions on how best to teach your children to pray. You must reach your own conclusions and formulate ideas to implement in your unique situation. I said at the beginning that we teach without a pedagogy, without a prescribed science of education, but by and large by ad-libbing our way through—"muddling," we might call it in our more honest moments. On the other hand, when we ask our Lord for wisdom, he does give it, just as he promised (James 1:5–6). If rearing children could be reduced to a formula, we would have heard long ago about such a marvel. Making our way through the maze is one of life's frustrations that we simply have to endure.

I do hope that through the course of this book you have had to ask yourself, "What, by the life that I live in their presence, am I teaching my children about prayer?"

You may wish that I had included more specifics, sure answers to problem situations. You may like books that tell you what to do and how to do it. They appear to be so much more practical. But are they? If the formulas don't exactly fit your situation, you're lost. *You* are the expert on your family, and I hope that the principles I've tried to spell out here will be just the guidance you need. You wouldn't be reading this book if you were not a parent who cares deeply about your children's spiritual development. I am confident that their spiritual lives will reflect that sincerity and that God will come to your aid whenever you ask him to.

Switch gears with me just for a moment as we conclude. Have you ever watched a spoked wheel? Try to picture one in your mind and then start that wheel turning—slowly at first then faster and faster. At first you can distinguish individual spokes, and the direction the wheel is turning is clear. But as the wheel picks up speed, the spokes begin to appear to be going in the opposite direction, and then they become a blur. Where do your eyes naturally go at that point? They are drawn to the hub, the center of the wheel, and it is there that you can determine the direction of the wheel.

When I began to think about this book, I thought I had a clear focus on all that I wanted to convey. I saw ten distinct areas that I wanted to touch on as they relate to the topic of teaching children to pray. I stated early on that my motivations were selfish in that I want my children's lives to be characterized by prayer. I want them to love the Lord as their mother and I do, and I desire that they enjoy the precious privilege of prayer with the same simple delight that I experienced as a child. As I wrote, the wheel moved faster and faster, spinning to the point where the spokes became a blur. It was not so much that I lost the sense of where the wheel was turning as much as I lost the sense of what this wheel was all about. I intended this book to be about my children and suddenly found it was convicting me. And I had to refocus on the hub.

I became frustrated that no matter how I began a chapter I found myself returning to one central recurring theme, *discipleship*. You also will find that regardless of where you begin in this endeavor of teaching your children to pray you will always return to the hub, this pivotal motif, discipleship. Paul said it without shame when he told others, "Follow my example, as I follow the example of Christ" (1 Corinthians 11:1).

Funny, isn't it? We began this journey together with a desire to teach our children to pray. Journey's end brings us to a different location altogether. Somewhere along this route my eyes drifted from the desire for my children to learn how to pray to examining my own life and *my* prayer. Though I began with young disciples calling, "Teach us to pray," I now return as a disciple to my Savior to ask that he teach me how to pray.

It seems that I have come full circle, but I have learned so many lessons along the route. My own prayer life has been enriched in the search for ways to enrich theirs.

So we conclude where we *should* have begun with a simpler request on our hearts, "Lord, teach us to pray."

> *I smile down at them, safe and warm,*
> *Snuggled deep into bed.*
> *And I thank you, Lord, for your gift of life,*
> *And kiss them gently on the head.*
>
> *As I turn to leave, only one thing more*
> *To make this picture complete:*
> *I want to know that their faith will grow*
> *Because, or in spite, of me.*
>
> *I want to teach them to pray, Lord,*
> *And help them listen for what you have to say.*
> *I want to show them they can trust you, Lord,*
> *And teach them to pray.*
>
> *My mind races with each step down the hall,*
> *Until I'm stopped by a precious sound.*
> *My little girl's talking to you, Lord,*
> *Like a special new friend that she's found.*
>
> *And I can't believe the sincerity,*
> *No rehearsed line or memorized phrase,*
> *Not the lofty words she's so often heard,*
> *Only simple words of perfect praise.*
>
> *So teach us to pray, Lord,*
> *To listen for what you have to say.*
> *Show us we can trust you, Lord,*
> *When our strength drains away.*
>
> *And teach us to love you, Lord,*
> *Teach us to love you, Lord;*
> *And teach us to pray.*[1]

Notes

Introduction

1. Robert Fulghum, *All I Really Need To Know I Learned in Kindergarten* (New York: Ivy Books, 1988), 4–5.

2. Bill Cosby, *Fatherhood* (Garden City, N.Y.: Dolphin Books, Doubleday, 1986), 65.

3. Ibid., 61.

4. Charlie Shedd, *Promises to Peter* (Waco: Word, 1970).

Chapter 1 My Father Taught Me To Pray

1. Quoted in Pat and Jill Williams, *Keep the Fire Glowing* (Old Tappan, N.J.: Revell, 1986), 59.

2. Bruce Wilkinson, "Third Generation Christians" (Moody Bible Institute Founders' Week Chapel Address), pt. 1, 1984.

3. Bill Cosby, *Fatherhood*, 158.

4. Michael Webb, "Lap Space in the Holy Place," *Discipleship Journal* 59 (1990): 62.

5. Jill Ellis, "Grandfather's Bible."

Chapter 2 Pattern Prayers

1. Adapted from Jill Briscoe, *Hush! Hush! It's Time To Pray* (Grand Rapids: Zondervan, 1978), 158.

2. Adapted from Alice D. Huff, World Intercessors School of Prayer (Greenwood, Ind.: OMS International, 1982), 8–9.

3. John M. Drescher, *If I Were Starting My Family Again* (Nashville: Abingdon, 1979). Quoted by Pat and Jill Williams, *Keep the Fire Glowing*, 42.

Chapter 3 When You Lie Down . . .

1. Edith Schaeffer, *L'Abri* (Wheaton, Ill.: Tyndale, 1969), 53.

2. *Pulpit Helps* (Chattanooga, Tenn.: Ministry of AMG International).

3. Ernest Lewis, *Light for the Journey* (Waco, Tex.: Word, 1986), 85.

4. Pat and Jill Williams, *Keep the Fire Glowing*, 58.

Chapter 4 Building Their Faith

1. Jane Fitz-Randolph, "Mr. Reid Does the Trees." Originally published in *The Christian Science Monitor*, Nov. 7, 1984. Reprinted here with permission from the April 1985 *Reader's Digest*.

2. Wesley L. Duewel, *Mighty Prevailing Prayer* (Grand Rapids: Zondervan, 1990).

Chapter 5 Making Prayer Understandable Without Making It Trite

1. Judith Frost Stark, *Don't Cross Your Bridge Before . . . You Pay the Toll* (Los Angeles: Price Stern Sloan, 1982). Condensed in *Reader's Digest* (December 1985): 113.

2. Eutychus, *Christianity Today*.

3. *Creative Bible Learning for Children* (Ventura, Calif.: Regal, 1977).

Chapter 6 Prayer of Salvation

1. "Fowler on Faith," *Christianity Today* (June 13, 1986), 7-I.

2. Wes Haystead, *Teaching Your Child About God* (Ventura, Calif.: Regal, 1983), 115.

3. Julie Stump, materials for Kids' Connection (1990), 342 N. Walnut St., Union City, Ohio 45390.

Chapter 7 Prayer Etiquette

1. Elizabeth L. Post, "Etiquette for Everyday," *Good Housekeeping* 5 (November 1990): 52.

2. Kari Torjesen Malcolm, *Building Your Family to Last* (Downers Grove, Ill.: InterVarsity, 1987), 65.

Chapter 8 Letting Them Touch Their World Through Prayer

1. Karen Burton Mains, *Open Heart—Open Home* (Elgin, Ill.: David C. Cook, 1976).

2. Edith Schaeffer, *L'Abri*, 16.

3. Gloria Ichikawa, *Moody Monthly* (January 1984): 76–77.

Chapter 9 Praying for Your Child

1. Wayne Watson, "Somewhere in the World" (Waco, Tex.: Word Records, 1985). From the album *Giants in the Land*.

2. Ray Boltz, "Jesus, Here's Another Child" Waco: Word Records, 1990.

Afterword

1. Sherri Wooden, "Teach Us to Pray." © 1991.